THE BEST OF SPORTS
GRAPHIC DESIGN
AND BRANDING

GINGKO PRESS

**THE BEST OF SPORTS
GRAPHIC DESIGN AND
BRANDING**

First Published in the USA and in Europe in 2019 by

GINGKO PRESS

Gingko Press, Inc.
2332 Fourth Street Suite E
Berkeley, CA 94710 USA
Tel: (510) 898 1195
Fax: (510) 898 1196
Email: books@gingkopress.com
www.gingkopress.com

Gingko Press Verlags GmbH
Schulterblatt 58
D-20357 Hamburg / Germany
Tel: +49 (0)40-291425
Fax: +49 (0)40-291055
Email: gingkopress@t-online.de

ISBN 978-3-943330-22-9

By arrangement with
Sandu Publishing Co., Ltd.

Copyright © 2019 by Sandu Publishing
First published in 2019 by Sandu Publishing

Sponsored by Design 360° — Concept & Design Magazine
Edited and produced by Sandu Publishing Co., Ltd.
Book design, concepts & art direction by Sandu Publishing Co., Ltd.

Chief Editor: Wang Shaoqiang
Executive Editors: Maxine Chang, Zhang Zhonghui
Copy Editor: Kim Curtis
Designer: Liu Xian
Sales Manager: Deng Baoyi

Cover Design by Wu Yanting
Front cover projects by José Maria Cunha, Wall-to-Wall Studios
Back cover projects by Studio WillemsPeeters, José Maria Cunha,
ReflexDesign

info@sandupublishing.com
sales@sandupublishing.com
www.sandupublishing.com

Printed and bound in China

CONTENTS

Events & Teams

PREFACE

The X Factor of Sports Design

By Rafael Esquer

The Bayankhongor Province in southwestern Mongolia is about as remote as you can get. The airport in its tiny capital city has two runways. One of them is paved. On the semi-desert steppes that spill away from the city, plains and mountains extend as far as the eye can see. It seems like a land forgotten in time. Yet, in this extreme corner of the world, on the wall of a cave burrowed into the arid-cold steppes, a painting from the Neolithic age depicts one of the most human endeavors—the ageless ritual of sport. Two wrestlers, locked in an embrace, perform for a crowd of spectators.

Sports would not exist without fans and fans would not exist without the promise of entertainment. And what was true 9,000 years ago, is still true today: Every successful element of design for sports must deliver this entertainment factor for the fans.

To me, the modern age of sports kicked off in 1930 with the first FIFA World Cup tournament. Since then, the sports industry has grown into the multibillion-dollar global juggernaut we recognize today. Without question, sports is now the world's most exciting form of entertainment. Our passion for sports has spread across many media: TV, film, social media, gaming, advertising, art, fashion and, of course, design. Undoubtedly, new technologies and media will open even more platforms for sports and sports design in the future. For the graphic designer, the breakneck pace of change in sports is dizzying—and daunting. What keeps your inspiration fresh and flowing? What becomes your North Star for branding when the world spins so fast?

My inspiration goes all the way back to this painting in the Bayankhongor cave. It is not that the Bayankhongor cave painting is the oldest example of "graphic design" for a sport. The famous Lascaux caves in France, for example, also contain painted scenes of wrestling and sprinting, and date back even further by 6,000 years. But for me, what captures my attention in the Bayankhongor cave painting is that, as far as I know, it is the first depiction of a sporting event with spectators. Here we see a marked shift from sport as ritual or physical conditioning for hunting or war to the prehistoric emergence of sport as entertainment. Yes, 9,000 years ago, Bayankhongor had wrestlers. But those wrestlers also had fans.

Let's remember that "fan" is short for fanatic from the Latin fānāticus meaning of "a temple, inspired by a god." Fans give the sports industry its competitive edge. While many other businesses have customers, the sports industry has adrenaline-seeking, die-hard fans. Vivek Ranadivé, co-owner and chairman of the NBA's Sacramento Kings describes it well, "Fans will paint their face purple, fans will evangelize... Every other CEO in every business is dying to be in our position—they're dying to have fans."

But Ranadivé tells only one side of the story. For sports designers, the stakes are higher. Fans have the power to make or break a design. If the sports design is embraced, it becomes not just part of the team's identity, but the fans' identity as well. On the very same day the New York City Football Club launched its badge with its iconic white monogram against a rich obsidian blue, photos from fans, flashing fresh tattoos of the design, flooded social media. It is worth noting, at that time, the New York City Football Club hadn't yet signed a single player or even secured a stadium. On the other hand, if the design is rejected by fans, this can lead to dire consequences. In 2013, when Everton Football Club in the Premier League in England launched a new badge presenting a modernized version of their iconic St. Rupert's Tower, within hours, tens of thousands of fans had circulated and signed a petition protesting the new design. One week later, the fan power was felt. Officials of Everton apologized profusely and pledged to go back to the drawing board. And they did. The new badge was used in only one season and was replaced the next season with a fan-approved design.

Let it be known when it comes to the design, the presence and power of the fans make all the difference.

With so much at stake, though, how do we decode the phenomenon of sports and create a design that represents the essence of the team and its avid spectators? To me, sports can be distilled into three essential factors: the athletes, the fans and that ineffable factor, the entertainment. For a designer, the key word here is entertainment, that magical link between fan and athlete. A successful sports design must evoke the entertainment factor, otherwise you're in for the Everton problem. So, what goes into a successful sports design? Simultaneously, it must feel exciting and friendly, heroic and approachable, seductive and memorable, classic and fresh. When I was asked to rebrand the NBA's Houston Rockets and launch the new badge design for the MLS's New York City Football Club, I approached these projects with this foremost in mind—how can I best capture that unique quality of entertainment and the interplay between fan and athlete, place and team? I approached the design process seeing the possibility of design ideas from many angles and asking myself many questions. I became the TV camera that trains its eye on the game, curious to see: Will the design have synergy on TV? I became the player: Will the design make me look and feel like a winner? I became the team owners: Will the new brand sell tickets, move merchandise and fill stadiums? I became a storyteller: Will the new brand tell a persuasive story? I became the number one fan: Will the design give me a sense of pride and belonging with the new team? Is the new logo strong enough to make me a brand ambassador? Most importantly, I stayed true to the overarching mission of sports, asking: Does the new brand have that desired entertainment factor?

The Bayankhongor cave painting is an eternal reminder to me that sports would not exist without the fans and the fans wouldn't exist without the entertainment. The Bayankhongor cave wrestlers wear no branding and neither do their spectators indicate their affiliation. But when I look at this painting, I see the kinetic energy, the surge of adrenaline, the flow of affiliation that the fans and athletes get from one another. This is the magic of sports. In today's world, the designer is in charge of visualizing this magic. And great sports design, in whatever medium or style, must honor, capture and contribute to just that.

APPAREL & EQUIPMENT

Futura

Futura is an independent, multi-disciplinary design agency based in Johannesburg, South Africa. They create concepts, experiences, interactions and communication for a new generation of consumers.

"We exist to drive innovation in sports design. Convention is the enemy."

1. In 2018, you did several sports design projects. What process do you follow when you start a project?

We always start with the athlete. We believe that to successfully portray an insightful sport-inspired work, one must understand and speak to the athlete first.

2. You did many creative designs for Nike. What were the advantages and limitations of working with such a well-known sports brand, especially when it has a clear branding strategy?

The advantages of working with Nike, for any design studio, is the brand's appetite for innovative and groundbreaking work. Even though there are brand guidelines in place, we are never limited by them and are always in a position to adapt them to better suit us locally.

3. You helped the Kaizer Chiefs Football Club to launch a set of equipment to a younger market. In your opinion, what does the younger generation want from sports visual design?

Sport and culture have merged. As a younger generation, we want to see sport as insightful, creative and visually appealing as other popular culture work. Secondly, we are far more critical of work being authentic. If the work is authentic and true, it will resonate with younger consumers.

4. Let's talk about color. How did you settle on the different shades of yellow for the Hail The Chief and The Joburg Force Workshop?

Yellow is the Kaizer Chiefs club's color. Gold is our city—Johannesburg's color. For Hail The Chief, we worked with hundreds of shades of yellow and gold to emulate the club and its strong connection with our city. The Joburg Force Workshop's colors were very much inspired by the yellows in

construction and workwear with "Respect the Work" being the overarching theme.

5. Font always plays an important role in sports graphic design. What trends have you seen since you did so well in choosing the right font for your projects?

Typography is a cornerstone of our design process. The choice of typography should be meaningful before anything else. It must connect conceptually with the project. The aesthetics should be inspired by function, legibility and timelessness.

6. There are many conventions in sports visual design. How did you deal with the relationship between innovation and those conventions?

We exist to drive innovation in sports design. Convention is the enemy.

7. In the project, The Joburg Force Workshop, you were required to lead customers to focus on Air Force 1. What did you do to achieve this goal?

Instead of just showing people the Air Force 1 story, we invited them to take part in the creation of their own version of the timeless silhouette of Air Force 1.

8. We know that design trends are influenced by culture, art, technology and so on. In your opinion, what in particular affects today's sports visual design?

Now, more than ever, sport is a unifying force that inspires everyday people to move beyond their boundaries. Designs should emulate this impact. They should be inspirational, innovative, aspirational and uplifting.

The Joburg Force Workshop

‣ Sneaker Customization Studio

‣ DESIGN AGENCY **Futura**
‣ CONSTRUCTION **C76,**
  Blue Cube Construction
‣ EVENT PARTNERS **Witch Wizard**
  Productions, Black Faff

In 2018, Futura was engaged in developing the brand touchpoint for The Force Workshop, Africa's first official Air Force 1 customization studio, during Capsule Fest 2018, one of the biggest street culture festivals in Johannesburg. The client emphasized it was imperative that Air Force 1 was the main product feature. Futura used customization to tap into the creative energy of the city. Hundreds of purpose-made elements were produced to assist in customizing the Air Force 1. This was done in an interactive space made up of 90 yellow shipping crates and industrial oil drums, which drew inspiration from the utility aesthetic and the latest version of Air Force 1.

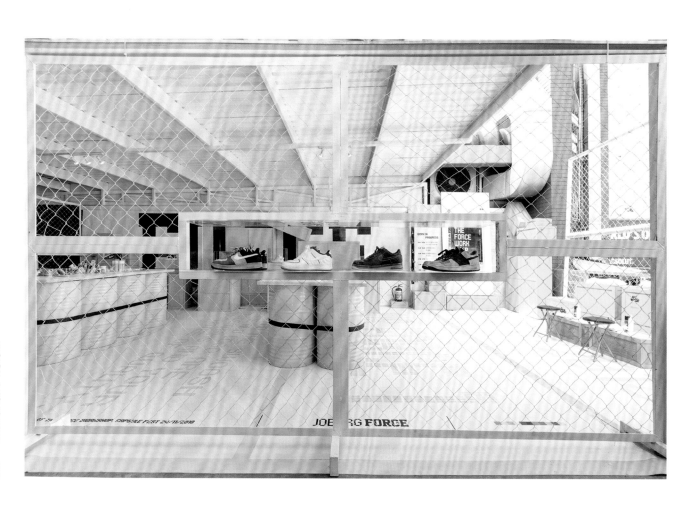

Hail The Chief. Kaizer Chiefs Kit Launch

▸ Team Kit

▸ DESIGN AGENCY **Futura**
▸ STYLING **Chloe Andrea**
▸ PRODUCTION **Lampost Productions**
▸ POST PRODUCTION **JP Hanekom,
 Swansong Post**
▸ PHOTOGRAPHY **Travys Owen**

In 2018, Futura was commissioned by Nike to launch the new kit for Kaizer Chiefs, a South African football club, to a younger market with a focus on both female and male fans and, at the same time, help position the club in the minds of South African youth as a powerhouse in local football. Futura developed the club's motto "Hail The Chief" along with a manifesto that spoke to the hearts and minds of fans, players and past heroes of Kaizer Chiefs Football. Futura developed a visual language for the club, drawing on its rich cultural heritage. "Hail to the ones who came first, the authors of our glamour. Hail to the fearless ones, the keepers of our glory. Hail to the true believers. Hail you, The Chief."

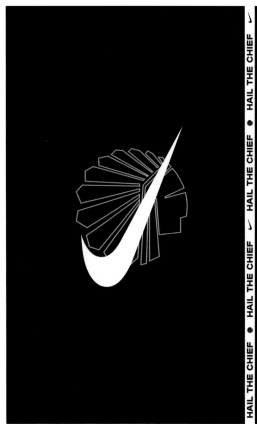

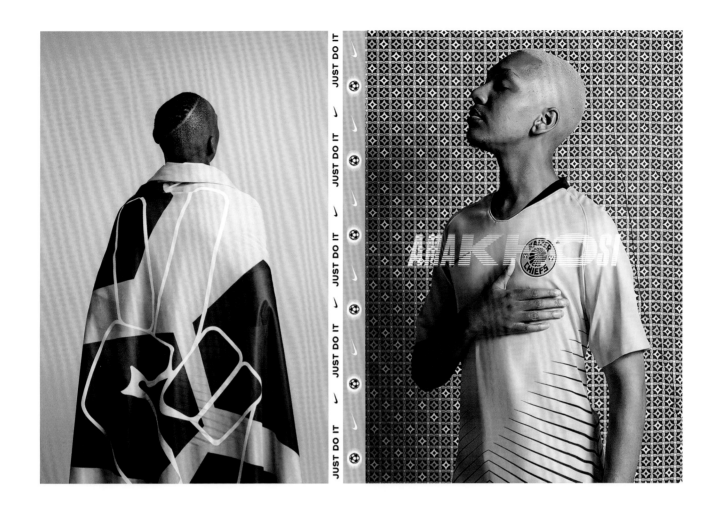

theLAB108

▸ Apparel Brand

▸ DESIGN **Tyodi Hyojin Lee**
▸ CLIENT **the LAB108**

theLAB108 is a multipurpose shop that develops various brands from the concept of "athleisure" and introduces these brands to women in their 20s to 40s. Its brand design started from "108." Inspired by the meaning of "108," the brand identity is drawn as a stable column with relaxed margins and repeating straight and curved lines. The overall communication of the brand is drawn from the marbling, expressing infinite beauty and the unification of mental and physical health.

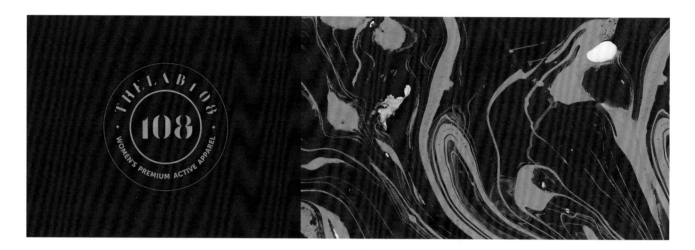

▲ "1" stands for the unification of mental health and physical health based on psychological realization. "0" stands for the emptying and calming of the mind. "8" stands for infinite beauty.

theLAB108 has a deeper meaning. The number 108 derives from significance in many eastern religions. 108 is a number known to refer to spiritual completion. 1 being the one, 0 representing emptiness and finally 8 meaning infinity. We, Women, through active and healy mind and body, want to reach taht nirvana and thelab108 will help you reach that goal in style.

The Athlete's Foot

▸Footwear Retailer

▸ DESIGN AGENCY **Re Agency**
▸ DESIGN **Floriane Jambu**
▸ CREATIVE DIRECTION **Colin Cornwell**
▸ DESIGN DIRECTION **Daniel Ioannou**
▸ CLIENT **The Athlete's Foot**

Established in 1981, The Athlete's Foot is the largest retailer of athletic footwear in Australia and is known for its quality products and knowledgeable staff. Re was commissioned to rebrand it to inspire a new generation of athletes. Re's solution was to put the technical details front and center, taking precision and data as their visual and verbal language. The brand system was underpinned by two grids that could scan, annotate and highlight information, showcasing the brand's in-depth knowledge of product and fit.

▴ Re also helped launch MyFit Pod, a fitness tracker, and its partner app.

Innvictus

▸ Retail Store

▸ DESIGN AGENCY **Brands&People**
▸ ART DIRECTION **Melanie Barajas, Gil Cornejo**
▸ IDEATION **Eduardo Jara, Christian Martínez**
▸ PRODUCTION **Nobody and Underdog**
▸ INNVICTUS TEAM **Armando López, Sergio Porras**

Brands&People was commissioned by Innovasport, the biggest sporting goods retailer in Mexico, to create a new identity, and later, a communication strategy for their new company, Innvictus, that specialized in bringing the best and latest sneakers to consumers. Brands&People designed a clean and in-your-face identity, all-caps, black and white. The square, which enclosed the name, gave the designers room to play with different applications, while also representing being on a basketball court.

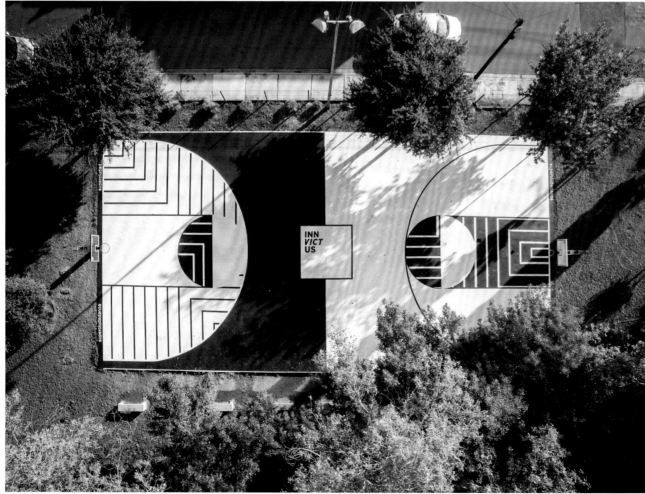

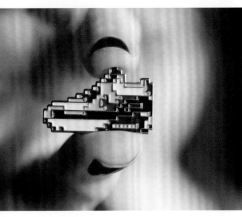

Nike, NBA, Fall 2017

▸ T-shirts

▸ DESIGN AGENCY **My Name Is Wendy**
▸ CLIENT **Nike NBA**

My Name Is Wendy was selected with other agencies to redesign the NBA practice T-shirts. Their task was to create a bold and audacious design through typography that would be used for the shirts. Each design needed to be modular enough to be adapted to all 30 NBA teams.

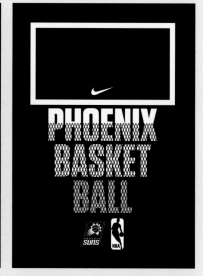

Nike Track + Field 2016

▸ Nike's Clothing Line

▸ DESIGN AGENCY **Studio.Build**
▸ CLIENT **Nike Track + Field**

Studio.Build was commissioned to create a bold, dynamic and engaging identity for Nike's 2016 Track + Field line. They designed a super-bold visual identity system, which took its cues from markings used on running tracks and sports fields.

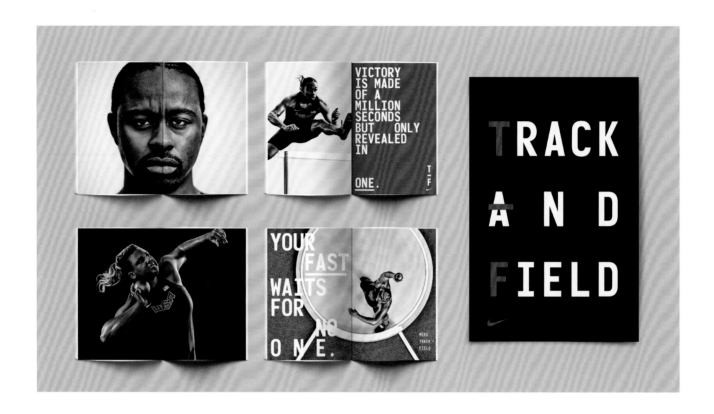

NIKE
TRACK +
FIELD

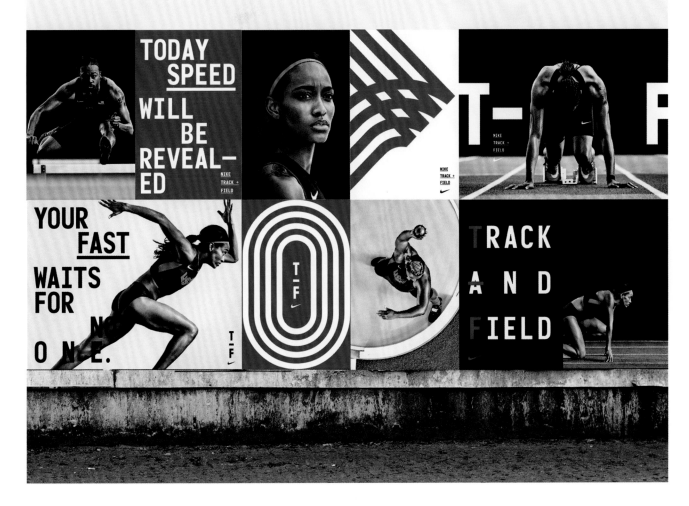

Nike Track + Field 2018

▸ Nike's Clothing Line

▸ DESIGN AGENCY **Studio.Build**
▸ CLIENT **Nike Track + Field**

In 2018, Studio.Build continued to design fresh and punchy visual identity systems for Nike's Track + Field line. The refreshed identity needed to stay in line with the original lockups and logos they created in 2016. They built on the initial work created for Track + Field 2016 by creating additional graphics for the visual center and updating the color palettes. The graphics were inspired by the graphics used on athletic fields.

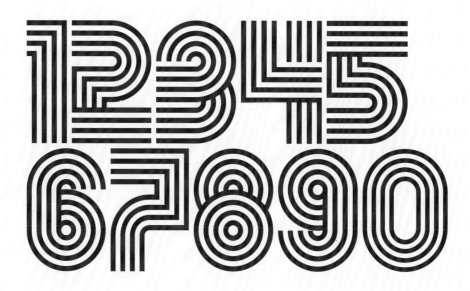

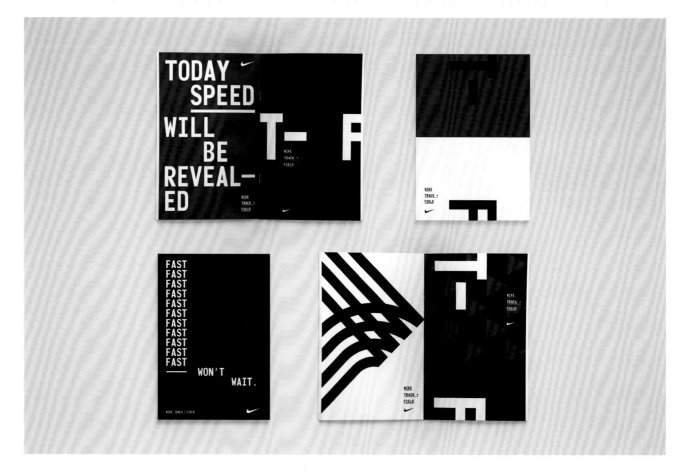

COSM

‣ Clinic

‣ DESIGN AGENCY **ED.**
‣ DESIGN **Cam Tidy**

Canberra Orthopaedics and Sports Medicine (COSM) is a clinic focused on getting people back on their feet, so they can keep doing the sport they love. The brand is focused on the results of the service: keep on running, keep on skiing, keep on climbing. The brand is versatile enough to be targeted at specific campaigns. The brand had to be fun, friendly and keep the patient's mind on the positive outcomes as medical treatment can be quite intimidating.

JimJams

▸ Apparel Brand

▸ DESIGN AGENCY **Anagrama Studio**
▸ PHOTOGRAPHY **Caroga Foto**

JimJams is a brand specializing in garments with designs, including sports personalities and recent sporting events. Its logo was based on strategic play diagrams commonly used by coaches, giving the brand a dynamic and cheerful communication style. The custom typeface is printed with textured strokes and establishes a brand personality that plays fairly with the garment designs. The typographic system includes the Effra and Univers LT families. The brand pattern and the elements that make up this project aesthetically communicate the guiding concept behind the brand—sports.

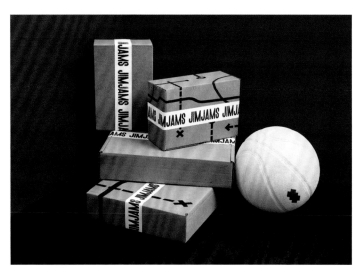
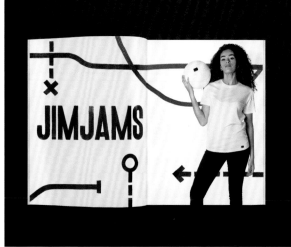

JIMJAMS

LEBRON JAMES SAVE THE KING CAMISETA

$420 MXN   Últimas Piezas

DESCRIPCIÓN   MATERIALES

La playera JimJams de Lebron James para mujer Save The King cuenta con tecnología Dri-FIT para mantenerte seco y cómodo, ya sea que estés corriendo en la cancha o representando a tu jugador favorito.

ESCOGE TU TALLA   S   M   L   XL   XXL

CANTIDAD   −   1   +

Guía de tallas / **Precios de envío**

AGREGAR AL CARRITO   AGREGAR A WISHLIST ♡

Knapper

▸ Equipment Manufacturer

▸ DESIGN AGENCY **byHAUS**
▸ DESIGN **Philippe Archontakis, Martin Laliberté**
▸ SOUND DESIGN **Underground**
▸ INDUSTRIAL DESIGN **Louis-Martin Beauséjour**
▸ PHOTOGRAPHY **Simon Duhamel**

byHAUS was commissioned to refresh the identity and gear of Knapper, an equipment manufacturer exclusively dedicated to street hockey. byHAUS redesigned the logo by drawing a single continuous movement. It then influenced the graphic expression for all the building blocks of the brand, including colors, typography, photographic stylistics and the production of all the products. The new identity was designed with the clear intention to make Knapper the new milestone of this sport.

VOLT Padel

▸ Padel Rackets Brand

▸ DESIGN AGENCY **VOLTA Brand Shaping Studio**

Padel, a game of tennis played between walls, is booming in Portugal. The client wanted to take advantage of this boom and show itself as the first Portuguese brand of padel rackets and gear. They asked VOLTA to create a brand that would set them apart from other padel rackets. VOLTA created the naming and concept behind VOLT's padel brand design. They chose "voltage" for its name and visual identity, and created a simple and clean look that inspired speed, agility and confidence.

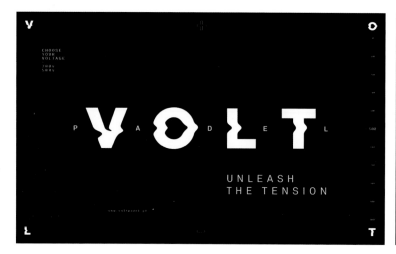

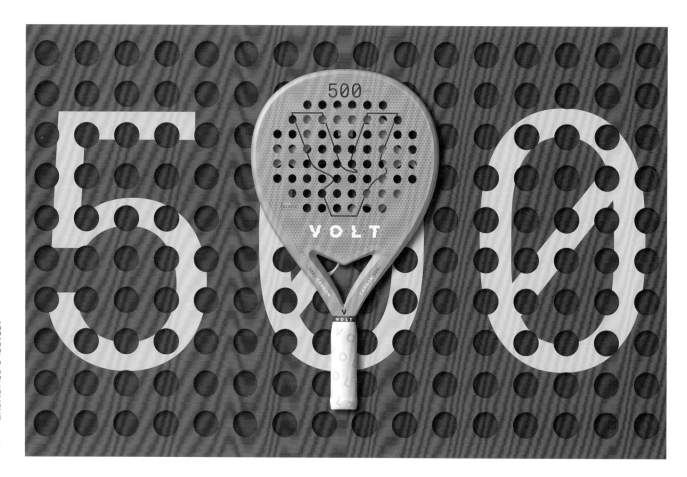

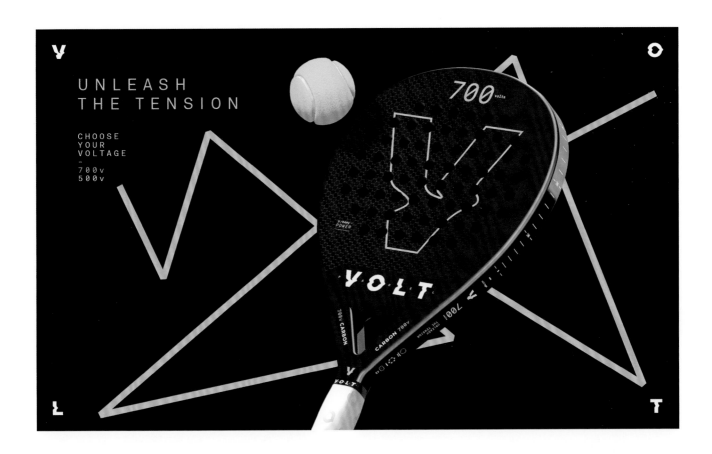

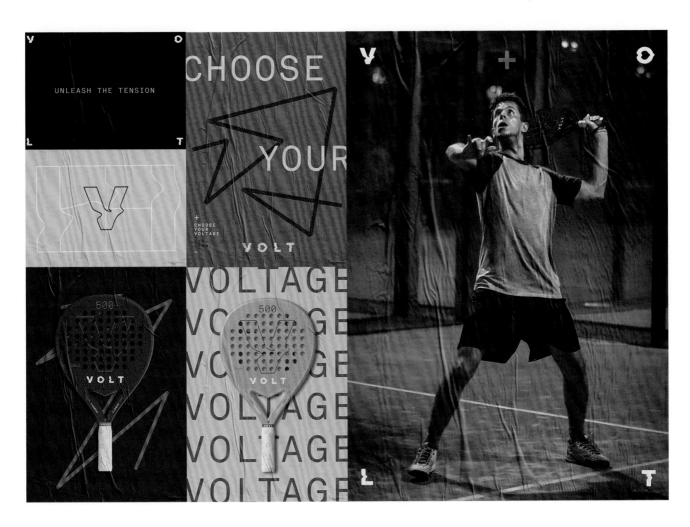

Nomad

▸ Sports Chalk Brand

▸ DESIGN AGENCY **Heavy**
▸ ART DIRECTION **Lane Cope, Sofía Vargas**

Nomad is a brand of sports chalk in the Philippines that imbues people with the gripping strength of 10 gorillas. Heavy was commissioned to create the branding for a sports chalk that would break the mold and be visually compelling to a Millennial audience. Their tasks included naming, brand identity, auxiliary graphics, and packaging for powder, block and chunky. Heavy's visual approach was inspired by vintage typeface combinations, using varied bold and playful fonts for impact. They used a stony texture in a black and white color scheme to reflect the mineral nature of the product with primary color accents for each variation.

VRYNK

‣Sportswear Store

‣DESIGN AGENCY ©N7 STUDIO
‣DESIGN Jaime Lomelin
‣CREATIVE DIRECTION Victor Celaya, Jaime Lomelin

VRYNK is an active sportswear store based in New York City. Through their brand, they sought to achieve visual communication that would set them apart from the rest. VRYNK was not only looking to impress the market, but to influence it. ©N7 STUDIO created a conceptual branding that would remain memorable and strong. They defined the brand, philosophy, message and style to correspond to a powerful manifesto that would become the brand's DNA. The visual identity of the brand embodies the combination of sportswear and streetwear. The result was a brand for the bold and the fearless.

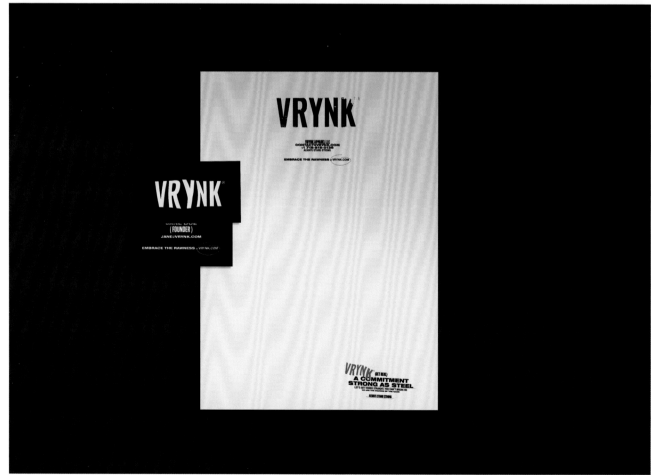

Alter Ego Sneaker Boutique

‣ Retail Store

‣ DESIGN AGENCY **Forth + Back**
‣ CLIENT **Alter Ego**

Alter Ego is a sneaker boutique based in Los Angeles. The shop owner sought to honor the memory of a friend who had fueled his passion for sneakers. With this in mind, Forth + Back developed a fictional dialogue between the owner and his friend that referenced the "second self" of a comic book superhero. This narrative drove everything from naming to interior graphics as well as all brand collateral.

Lodestar

▸ Apparel Brand

▸ DESIGN AGENCY **Crate47**

Crate47 was asked by the founders of Lodestar to create an original sports and lifestyle brand identity that would support their apparel in a competitive action sports market. Crate47 created the complete brand, including researching the sector, originating the name, and designing the logo and sub-branding. An essential part of the sub-branding was the chevron pattern, which was used on a variety of different labels, tags and packaging. The Crate47 team was also responsible for generating the artwork used on their T-shirts, embroidered badges and stickers. This included original illustrations and hand-drawn typography created by their in-house illustrator.

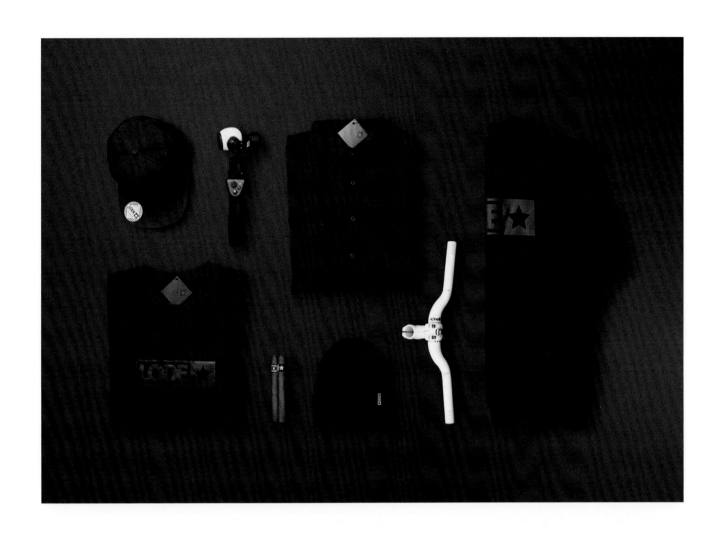

Form & Press

▸ Sports Apparel Brand

▸ DESIGN AGENCY **Departamento**
▸ DESIGN **Lucía González,
Paloma González**
▸ CREATIVE DIRECTION & ART DIRECTION
Erik Villarreal
▸ PHOTOGRAPHY **Karina Zertuche**

Departamento was commissioned to design a high-end brand that combined adventure, lifestyle, health and fitness. Form & Press is a clothing brand that revolves around fitness culture. Their products are constantly evolving and they apply the latest technology to their fabrics to improve the athletes' performance. The strategy to reflect this recurring evolution was to reflect both initials in merging form.

MONDAY-SUNDAY
9:00 — 22:00 × CT
LONDON, UK N°799
WWW.F-P.COM

FORM&PRESS

Messina Sans

Release: 2015

Designed by
LuziType®

ABCDEFGHIJKLMNÑOPQRSTUVWXY
abcdefghijklmnñopqrstuvwxyz
0123456789

store@f-p.com/ store@f-p.com/ store

Football Pro

▸ Retail Store

▸ DESIGN **Markos Zouridakis,
The Birthdays Design**
▸ CLIENT **Football Pro**

Football Pro is a retail store in Athens, Greece focused on football apparel. Markos Zouridakis and The Birthdays Design were commissioned to design the store's visual identity in a way worthy of the brands it hosted, while following and developing the already-existing identity. They developed a three-axis visual system of basic shapes and composing dynamics, a typographic system and a collage technique. The visual system was used in a variety of applications, such as panels, checkout counter background wall, posters, columns, etc. The common basis of all three is typography, action and emotion.

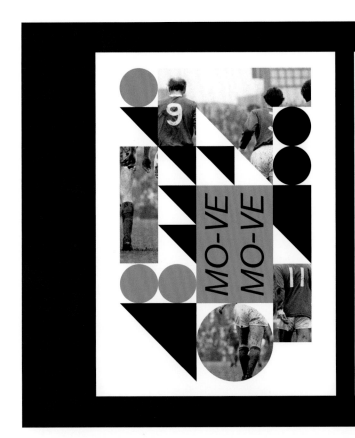

Two Feet Undr

‣ Retail Store

‣ DESIGN AGENCY **The Hungry Design Co.**
‣ ART DIRECTION **Ernesto Zamora**
‣ ILLUSTRATION **Moisés Córdova,
  Angel Puente**

The Hungry Design Co. created a mural for a sneaker shop in Monterrey, Mexico. Inspired by streetwear culture, they created a visual impact through graphics that represent three key points: sneakers, the street and graffiti. They designed a series of posters with contrasting palettes, and paint and spray to give them a street spirit. They were displayed in the store like propaganda, used on the street and given as gifts to customers.

Braid

‣ Sports Apparel Brand

‣ DESIGN **Marta Veludo**

Braid is a sportswear brand focused on the needs of women older than 35 that allows them to feel comfortable, confident and empowered on a daily basis, whether they are shopping, exercising, taking care of children, working or going out.

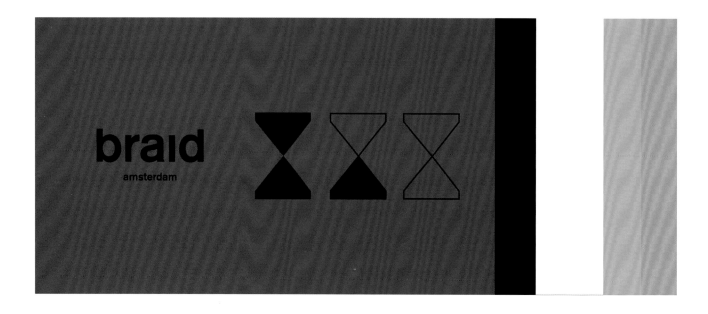

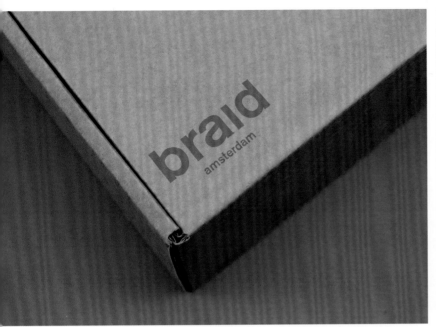

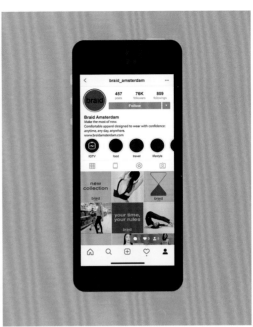

PUMA Duplex Sneaker Collaboration

‣ Sneaker

‣ DESIGN **Daniel Ting Chong**
‣ PHOTOGRAPHY **Nick Gordon**

Global sports brand PUMA collaborated with Cape Town, South Africa-based illustrator and designer Daniel Ting Chong to create two new sneaker iterations: a vintage Duplex OG and a modernized version of it, the Duplex Evo. Daniel created two distinctly African sneakers by drawing on traditional Zulu and Xhosa mythologies.

Miscellaneous Adventures

‣ Outdoor Brand

‣ DESIGN AGENCY **Misc Adventures Studio**

Miscellaneous Adventures is a collection of illustrations and graphics designed for the Miscellaneous Adventures outdoor brand.

An Ko Rau

‣ Sports Apparel Brand

‣ DESIGN AGENCY **702design**
‣ CLIENT **ZUCZUG**

702design was commissioned to create a new design concept of sport. The brand name "An Ko Rau" means "stationary" in Esperanto. The "o" graphic in the brand icon was inspired by a stopwatch timer, indicating that movement starts from stillness, ends at zero, then goes back around and begins again.

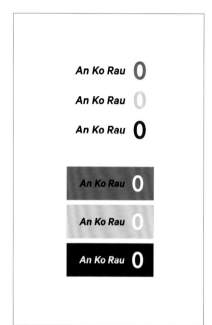

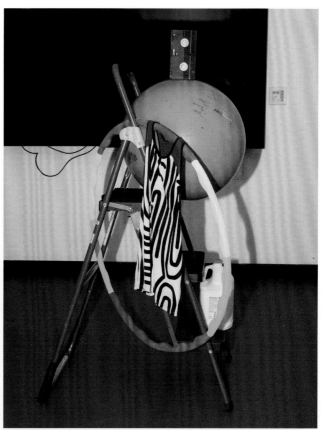

An Ko Rau 0

Ab Crew
▸ Fitness Products

▸ DESIGN AGENCY **ico Design**
▸ PHOTOGRAPHY **Ania Wawrzkowicz**
▸ CLIENT **Deciem**

ico Design was commissioned to create a brand and packaging for a new range of products targeted at male, body-conscious gym-goers. ico Design created a stylish, stripped-back aesthetic that echoes fitness heritage and gives the products instant stand-out across a range of different packaging formats from protein powder cans to shampoo bottles.

Uplift

▸DESIGN **José Maria Cunha**

The bodybuilding and fitness apparel brand Uplift needed a bold and strong brand that both top-tier athletes and sports fans could relate to. José Maria Cunha used a dynamic logotype to emphasize the effort and passion involved in high levels of competition.

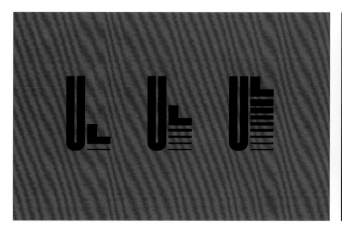

Ten Years of Shelflife

‣ Sneaker & Streetwear Store

‣ DESIGN **Daniel Ting Chong**
‣ APPAREL DESIGN **Daniel Bradley**
‣ STILLS DESIGN **James White**

Daniel Ting Chong was commissioned to create an apparel range celebrating Shelflife's 10th anniversary. He utilized the coordinates and contour lines from the original and new Shelflife stores on Loop Street and Longmarket Street as graphic devices. The color palette is that of Shelflife's branding, predominantly orange, black and white.

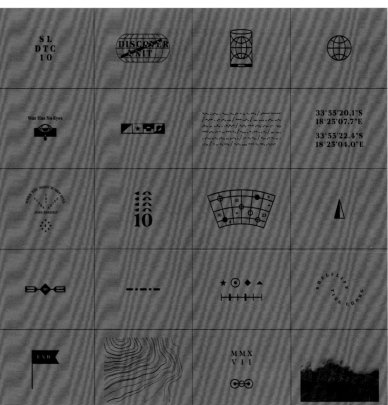

▲ The Morse code used in the repeated pattern is translated as "Celebrating 10 years of Shelflife. A collaboration between Shelflife and Daniel Ting Chong."

▴ Nike also celebrated this milestone by creating a unique pair of Air Max 1s for the collaboration.

Wattbike

▸ Indoor Training Bicycle Brand

▸ DESIGN AGENCY **Onwards**
▸ PHOTOGRAPHY **Michael Bodiam, Lulu Ash**

Indoor training bicycle brand Wattbike commissioned Onwards to renew their brand in an attempt to stand out from new competitors and connect with a new audience of amateur cycling obsessives. Detailed consumer research, interviews, competitor analysis and workshops revealed a core brand truth: Performance is everything. Onwards turned that insight into a single, purposeful idea, "Obsessed with performance," and translated it into a premium, yet highly technical brand identity system that takes visual cues from data.

Terinit

▸Sports Apparel Brand

▸DESIGN AGENCY **Ahonen & Lamberg**
▸CREATIVE DIRECTION **Rolf Ekroth**
▸STYLING **Tuomas Laitinen**
▸PHOTOGRAPHY **Osma Harvilahti**
▸CLIENT **Terinit**

Ahonen & Lamberg was commissioned to rebrand the Finnish heritage sportswear brand Terinit. The brand was established in 1949 and was widely popular in Finland throughout the 1980s for its skiing and ski jumping gear. The client wanted to renew the brand, while keeping close to its heritage. Drawing inspiration from image archives and the creative director's childhood memories, Ahonen & Lamberg created a unique visual identity. The logo is a combination of dynamism and boldness with a finely tuned letter design. It can be strongly used as a print on clothing. Along with the logo, the print designs play an important role in the new brand identity.

▴ Ahonen & Lamberg created a series of print designs, a playful mix of the sports imagery with hero prints like the Teeri-bird, which is related to the origin of the brand's name.

ŪNIMA – Active Soul Wear

▸ Sports Apparel Brand

▸ DESIGN AGENCY **Chapter Branding Studio**
▸ PHOTOGRAPHY **Alberto Pinto**
▸ CLIENT **ŪNIMA Active Soul Wear**

"Constantly on the move" has become a way of life for both the common city worker and fitness maniacs. ŪNIMA strives to merge these two worlds into garments fit for both. Chapter Branding Studio decided to give ŪNIMA a personality of its own by creating a bold logotype with a sober palette to communicate its determination and efficiency. The concept of soul is an important part of the project. It means that people are active not because they want to, but because they have to. An active soul is one that cannot stop trying to be better inside and out.

ASICS Tiger

▸ Sportswear Brand

▸ DESIGN AGENCY **Bruce Mau Design**
▸ TYPE DESIGN **Kontrapunkt**

The ASICS Tiger brand relaunched in 2015 as a platform for a contemporary sports lifestyle and was inspired by the company's iconic designs of the 1970s to 1990s. Bruce Mau Design developed a global brand identity system to implement across retail, digital and print points. Expanding from ASICS' seminal logo, this new brand identity acts as a link between the label's heritage and contemporary culture. The brand system is inspired by posters on the streets and applied through the use of bold brand photography layered over large-scale type. Bruce Mau Design worked with Kontrapunkt to develop a new typeface that merges the geometry of the ASICS logo with updated typographical components.

Nike Concept Store

▸ Retail Store

▸ DESIGN AGENCY **Oh Yeah Studio**
▸ TYPE DESIGN **Hans Christian Øren**
▸ STORE DESIGN **Thijs Pulles**
▸ ENVIRONMENTAL GRAPHIC DESIGN
  Joel Clifford
▸ ENVIRONMENTAL INSTALLATION
  Confetti Reclame

"Oslo" is a new custom typeface designed for the Nike Concept Store in Oslo, Norway. Nike wanted to use a local artist to create a narrative thread throughout the store. The brief required the creation of a bespoke typeface for the word "Oslo" and the sentence "Your only limit is you." Oh Yeah Studio created "Oslo," inspired by the Bislett Stadium, a place with a central role in Oslo's history as an international venue for sports and public festivals. The lines from the running track laid the foundation for the whole style. The font is used on the background of a whole wall, a big installation behind the counter and graphics throughout the store.

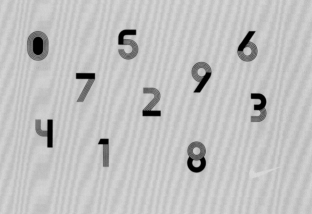

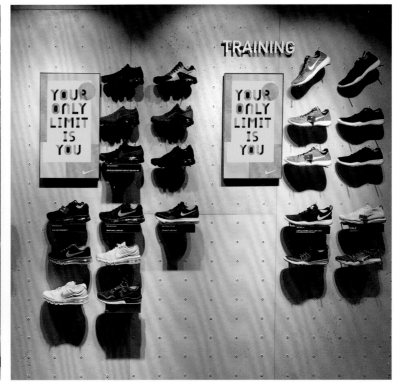

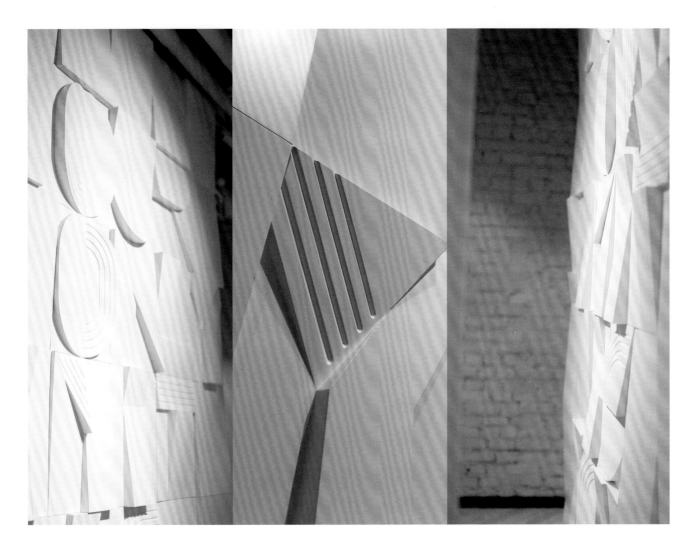

Strut This

▸ Apparel Brand

▸ DESIGN AGENCY **Lantern**
▸ CLIENT **Strut This**

Established in Los Angeles in 2011, Strut This is a fashion-focused activewear brand that creates premium performance clothing for women. They approached Lantern to update their branding and creative strategy. The new identity system is underpinned by a customized, versatile "st" ligature, which is shorthand for the brand name. The monogram then flexes to support a range of creative headlines. Seasonal lifestyle and product photography provides another important asset in the brand's armory. The new look was rolled out across marketing, social media, labels and packaging.

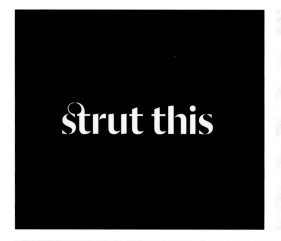

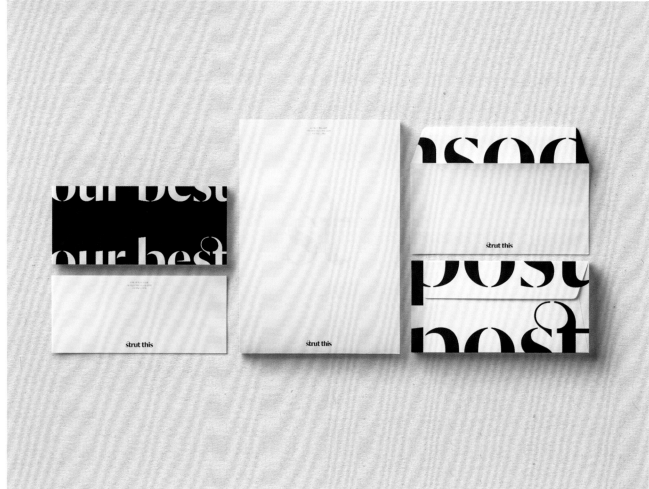

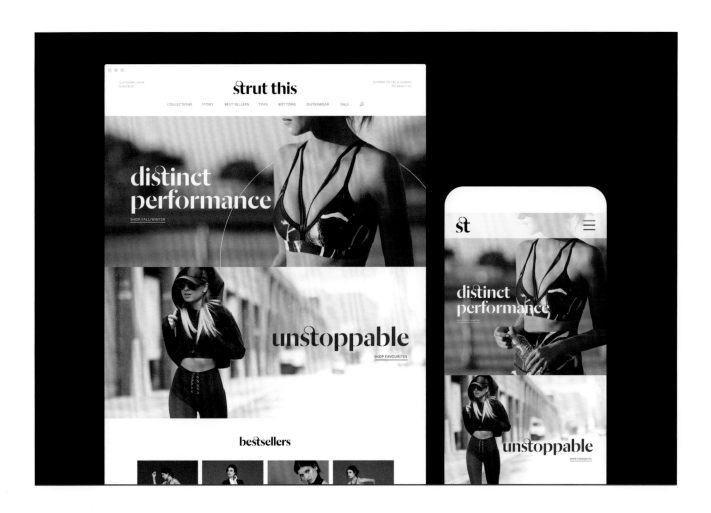

Play the Unplayable

▸ ASICS Tennis Campaign

▸ DESIGN **Marta Veludo**
▸ CONCEPT & CAMPAIGN DESIGN
  Greenroom Design Agency

Greenroom Design Agency commissioned Marta Veludo to create patterns, social media layouts and color explorations for the ASICS Tennis Campaign, "Play the Unplayable." They wanted the patterns, textures and edgy compositions to be inspired by the energy of the tennis players' movements and the game's border lines.

CLUBS & GYMS

Rosie Lee

"I'm really excited to see how sport will change to accommodate gender fluidity."

Rosie Lee is a creative agency with expertise in design, creative, digital and consultancy. It was founded in the UK in 2001 and now has four studios worldwide. Rosie Lee has rich experience in sports-related spatial design.

1. You did many spatial designs for Nike's campaigns. How did you conceive the design concepts for each campaign?

A lot of the time our inspiration comes directly from the product, the design of the product or the heritage behind it. We extract these stories and bring them to life in interesting ways, educating and engaging consumers.

2. What are the basic steps you take to start a spatial design project?

We think about the consumer experience, brand experience and touchpoints, shareable moments and site-specific details that really set one space apart from another. We try to localize as much as possible, to use the fabric of the building or material that roots it in the space. And we try to add personality with art and typography to resonate with the brand and to differentiate the experience from other stores.

3. How many people did you need to design and execute a project like the Air Max Day 2019 in Sanlitun (Beijing, China) or the London's Fastest at Tate Modern?

We focus heavily on recruitment and have an amazingly diverse talent pool at Rosie Lee, so, typically, we only need a team of five or 10 people to work on a project of this size. By keeping a strong, small team, we can work dynamically without sacrificing quality. The team does shrink and grow over the course of a project, depending on what the project needs.

4. You said that Corner Gym was "a completely blank canvas" for Rosie Lee. What were the differences between Corner Gym and your earlier projects?

Moscow is an exciting place and is evolving culturally with fantastic architecture and old buildings looking for someone to develop a fresh perspective for them. The client involved makes a huge difference. We work best with people who are passionate, trusting and brave. Our client is a great creative partner, incredibly progressive and well-travelled. He wants all the projects we work on with him to be not only the best in Moscow, but in the world.

The gym itself is in a totally unique space, an old bus garage, with loads of character and features. The trick was to work out what to dial up and what was needed practically to

make it a functioning, premium space. The brickwork of the building is amazing and we tried to keep as much exposed as possible. We used the middle wall panel to accentuate them as well as to serve as a pop of neutrality. We used programmable lights to change the mood, for example, to match the cardio moments, fight training, boxing matches or other events.

5. When you are doing a spatial design project, are the outcomes always consistent with the design? Please share with us your experiences.

Change is the only constant. We start with a vision and this helps us to pick the space or location, but sometimes things don't go to plan. It can be a very complicated discipline we work in, with many moving parts and sometimes things unrelated to the project can affect a direction or requirement, etc.

Holding a strong vision allows us to deal with anything that is thrown at us—the design may need to evolve, but the vision is always there showing us how we can make the most out of every challenge. Each project is different, some go to plan and others don't—but we always strive to achieve work we're proud of.

6. In your opinion, what kind of changes will be happening in the field of sports design with the application of the new media?

Sport is a fascinating subject and medium to work in, and there are many angles to explore. Change in sports design is not rooted to changes in any medium, but more from the creativity that can come from all its nuances—in disciplines and categories, to the emotions and experiences people have. Innovation and storytelling provide the biggest opportunities to rise to the challenges and changes in design. They are what bring audiences closer to sporting moments. Interpreting those and connecting them to the brands and products we work with is what always keeps the work interesting and evolving.

I'm really excited to see how sport will change to accommodate gender fluidity, too. At least 99.9 percent of sport is delineated between men and women, but that boundary is eroding very quickly outside of sport. The 2020 Olympics is fast approaching. Brands will be all over this topic, but will the Olympic Committee be able to move fast enough?

Corner

▸ Boxing Gym

▸ DESIGN AGENCY **Rosie Lee**

Rosie Lee was challenged to develop the concept for an all-new, premiere boxing gym in the heart of Moscow in what once housed an old bus depot. Their works ranged from creative concept, naming, style, visual identity and spatial design, to equipment, apparel design and, ultimately, to providing the blueprint for a future global expansion into the world of boxing. Influenced by the burgeoning new breed of fitness spaces and trends globally, Rosie Lee wanted to embrace the energy of the movement where the possibilities for these types of spaces were being re-imagined. The outcome was a place to train and to socialize, more akin to a nightclub than a spit-and-sawdust boxing gym.

▲ Rosie Lee created a dynamic core typographic style with onomatopoeic elements and bold visual graphic slogans to embrace the movement, attitude and actions associated with boxing.

DAF Assets

▸ Athletics Association

▸ DESIGN AGENCY **Rosie Lee**

Dansk Atletik, the Danish athletics association, approached Rosie Lee after projects they had worked on with Copenhagen running crew Wolfpack, to help them re-imagine their corporate visual identity. As sport and athletics have evolved, they wanted their identity to reflect this contemporary shift, embracing how athletes live both on and off the track. Their design focused on taking personal ownership of the track and offering the ability for it to morph into different expressions of athletic sport. By using the lines of the track, they were able to demonstrate these different disciplines, but also convey the movement and flow of the sport.

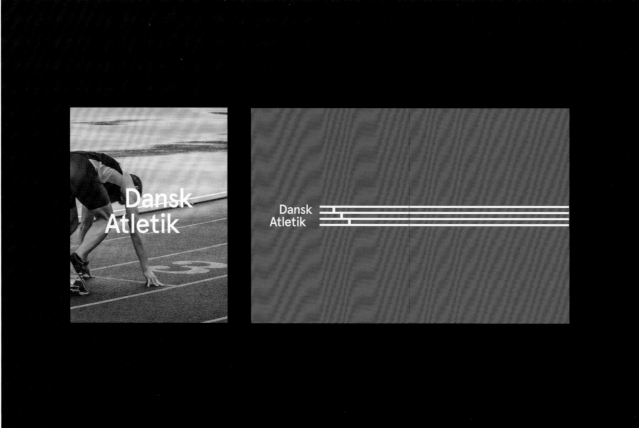

RE:UNION

▸Gym

▸DESIGN AGENCY **Frost*collective**
▸DESIGN **Kieran Mistry, Chris Griffiths, Molly Lewis**
▸CREATIVE DIRECTION **Vince Frost, Alex Dalmau**
▸BRAND STRATEGY **Jeanne Ogilvie**
▸ACCOUNT MANAGEMENT **Blayne Summergreene**
▸PHOTOGRAPHY **Tim Jones**
▸CLIENT **RE:UNION**

The RE:UNION program is designed to reshape how people understand fitness. Here, members work out together in teams of three and are matched up based on skill and ambition, using technology to track and focus activities in real time. Frost* was tasked with creating the naming, strategic identity, brand and communications, and interior concept for this exciting new brand.

REUNION®

RESET
RENEW
PREVENT

TRAIN TO THE POWER OF THREE

Ice Arena

‣ Skating Arena

‣ DESIGN **Jarosław Dziubek**
‣ CLIENT **Tomaszów Sports Center**

The Ice Arena Tomaszów Mazowiecki is the first indoor skating rink in Poland. It is a multi-functional facility for speed skating, figure skating, ice hockey and short track. The logo was inspired by the shape of the ice rink. The strong sign is adaptive to both international skating competitions and local events for residents. The responsive logo, supported by strong typeface, gives dynamics to the whole brand identification.

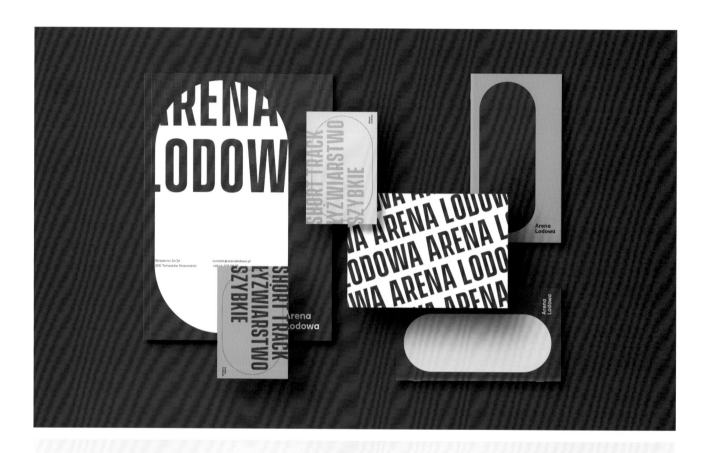

Arena
Lodowa

Arena
Lodowa

Arena
Lodowa

The Aquatic Club

‣ Swim Club

‣ DESIGN AGENCY **Estudio Yeyé**
‣ ART DIRECTION **Orlando Portillo**
‣ CLIENT **The Aquatic Club**

The Aquatic Club is a swim club with music and food in Las Vegas, Nevada. With a stylish nod to the intimate, yet energetic environment of social and racquet clubs of decades past, The Aquatic Club offers a posh atmosphere like no other in Las Vegas. The lines used as a pattern are classic and inherently related to swimsuits, especially 1950s fashion when the trend to use high contrasts began. This inspiration allowed Estudio Yeyé to generate a sexy and casual, yet chic brand.

SPECIALS

18 12 oz. cup 36 whole pineapple/watermelon cup
60 60 oz. pitcher 200 party tub vintage

VINTAGE

APEROL SPRITZ	Aperol, Prosecco, Soda Water
MOSCOW MULE	Belvedere, Fresh Lime, Ginger Beer
RUM PUNCH	Havana Club, Pineapple, Fresh Orange
FRENCH 75	Tanqueray 10, Lemon, Moët & Chandon Brut
EL DIABLO	Patrón Silver, Fresh Lime, Ginger Beer
RED/GREEN SNAPPER	Bombay Sapphire, Red or Green Tomato
	Fresh Lemon, Savory Garnish
FROST	Diving in to Hampton Water Rosé, Torani

CONTEMPORARY

THE WHITNEY	Hampton Water Rosé, Cointreau,
	Summer Berry Shrub, Prosecco
CITRINE	Patrón Silver, Grapefruit Syrup,
	Fresh Lime, San Pellegrino Pompelmo
TEE TIME	Absolut Lime, Shrub & Co Ginger,
	Cold Pressed Watermelon, Fresh Lime, Mint
FORTY LOVE	Cointreau, Passion Fruit, Fresh Lime,
	Fresh Orange, Moët Ice Rosé

REQUEST TO SEE OUR TREAT TRIKE
FOR A BOOZY POP REFRESHER

3

4

DON'T FORGET TO GET YOUR SNACKS

CHAMPAGNE 750 mL.	450
	450
Moët Ice Imperial	475
Moët & Chandon Brut Imperial	725
Veuve Clicquot Yellow Label	625
Dom Pérignon	475
Krug Grande Cuvée	700
Perrier-Jouët Brut	950
Perrier-Jouët Blanc de Blancs	975
Louis Roederer Cristal	
Ace of Spades	

BUBBLES

ROSÉ

Moët Ice Imperial Rosé	475
Dom Pérignon Rosé	1750
Veuve Clicquot Rosé	550
Ruinart Rosé	525
Roederer Cristal Rosé	1500
Perrier-Jouët Belle Epoque Rosé	1000

LARGE FORMAT

Moët & Chandon 3 liter	975
Veuve Clicquot 6 liter	3500
Dom Pérignon 1.5 liter	1500
Dom Pérignon 3 liter	5000
Dom Pérignon 6 liter	25000
Perrier-Jouët Belle Ep 1.5 liter	1500
Louis Roederer Cristal 1.5 liter	3000
Ace of Spades 6 liter	12500

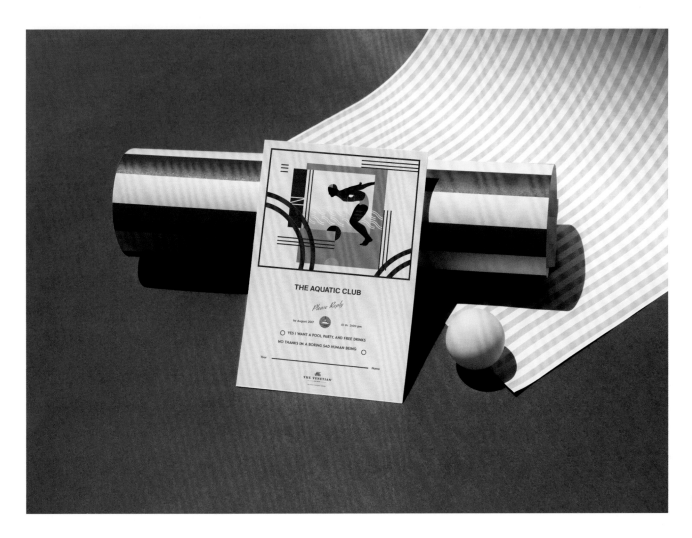

GO Park

> Sports Center

> DESIGN AGENCY **Apus Agency**
> DESIGN **Daniil Solosyatov**
> CREATIVE DIRECTION **Vitaly Afanasiev**
> ART DIRECTION **Vladimir Isaev**
> UI DESIGN **Alexey Yurasov**
> PHOTOGRAPHY **Dmitry Bulin**
> CLIENT **GO Park**

Apus Agency was faced with developing and launching a new brand for a major sports center in the Moscow area. The agency used the idea of motivation as the foundation of the brand. The agency suggested a laconic name, GO Park, which reflects the call to action. The agency's work includes naming as well as architectural design, and web and advertising materials.

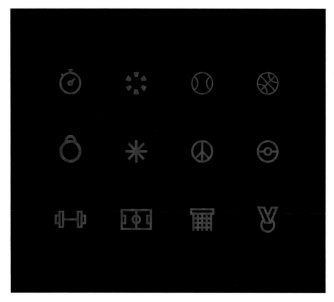

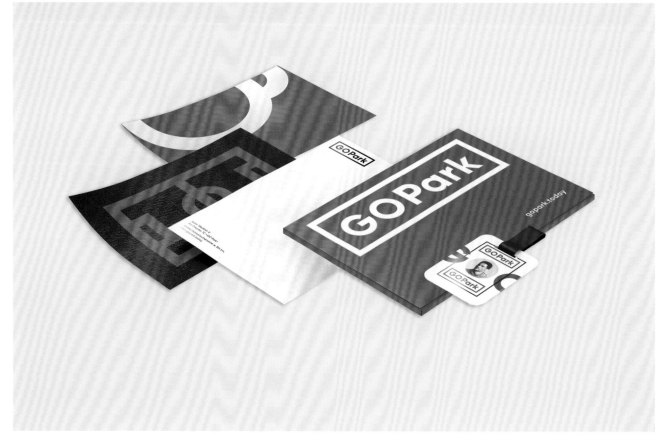

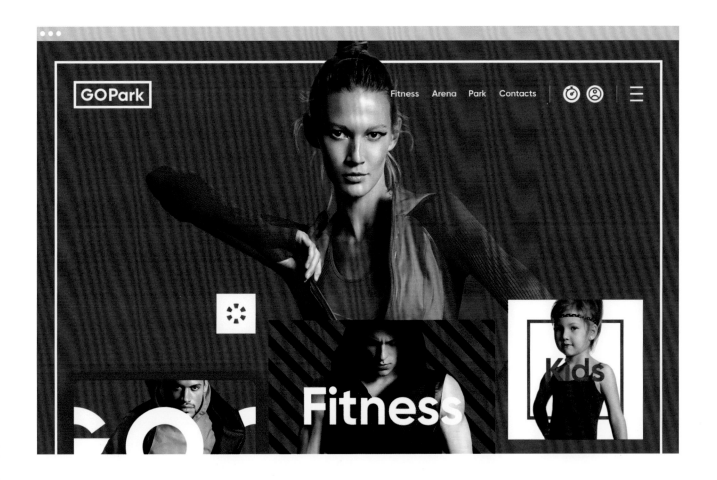

Big Bull CrossFit

▸ CrossFit Gym

▸ DESIGN AGENCY **Mano a Mano**

Big Bull is a new CrossFit gym in Matosinhos e Leça da Palmeira, Portugal. It's not an ordinary gym, but more of a sports club. It's about belonging to a community, training with other people and getting those results you want, while doing it as a team. The aim was to design a brand that would convey this spirit of family and team, collective effort, strength, and, above all, personality. This was achieved by designing an identity for not just its logo, but rather, for an entire lifestyle—from different bull's icons to quirky sentences that were then applied throughout the gym and other materials such as T-shirts and business cards.

Uncle Zhuo

▸ Weight Gain Gym

▸ DESIGN AGENCY **9 x 9. Design**

Uncle Zhuo is an Internet celebrity who focuses on working out. He pays more attention to those who want to put on weight. Therefore, in order to clearly express the concept of putting on weight, 9 x 9. Design adopted the concept of becoming stronger in its icon. The whole visual identity is based on retro comics. Leaving aside the traditional industrial style, it blends in more of a fashion feeling.

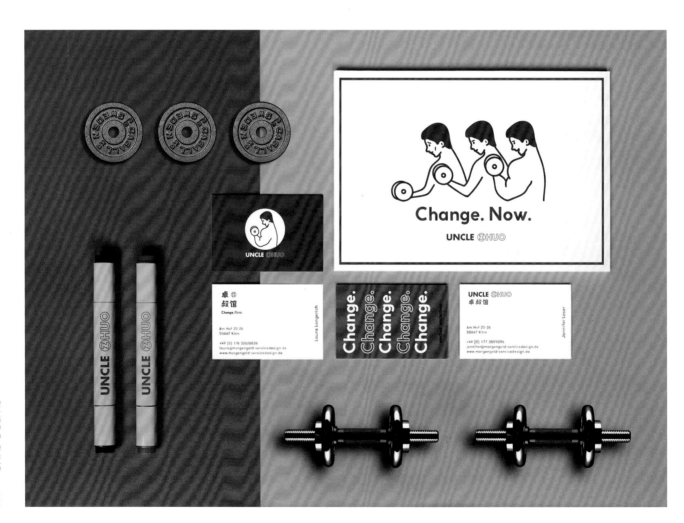

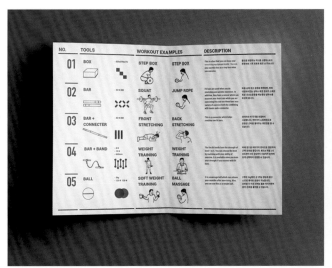

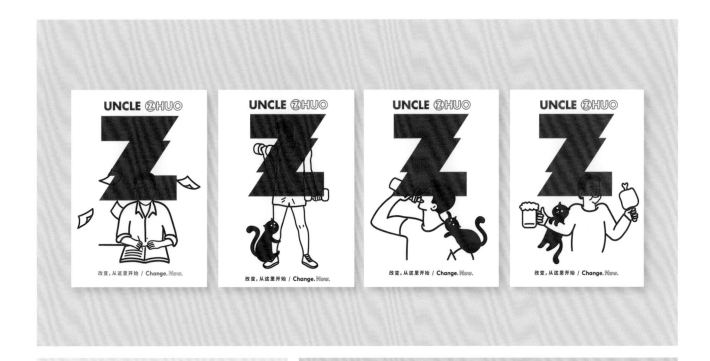

Dōjō

▸ Fitness Club

▸ DESIGN **Stepan Solodkov**
▸ CLIENT **Dōjō**

Dōjō is a fitness club located in Nairobi, Kenya. Stepan Solodkov's task was to create its identity in fusion style, combining the elements of traditional Japanese culture and Scandinavian minimalist design, and then add a slight accent from Africa. The identity is based on Dōjō's main motto: This is the path, the path to perfection. All graphics were made in black and white with only one additional color, red, which is common to the cultures of Japan and Africa. The minimalist design reflects the minimalist interior of the club.

Cell

▸ Functional Playground

▸ DESIGN AGENCY **Fable**
▸ DESIGN **Siokkan Chow, Marcus Gee, Isabel Tay**
▸ CREATIVE DIRECTION **Jiahui Tan**
▸ CLIENT **Cell**

Cell is a playground focused on both personal training and various group classes. The identity of Cell is based on the physiological truism that one has to break down one's muscles before building them up. Based on a singular grid, Fable designed a custom-stenciled typeface to represent grit, fight and strength. The typeface breaks up to form secondary patterns and graphics with accompanying designs that represent types of exercise like using kettlebells, battle ropes, practicing Pilates and more.

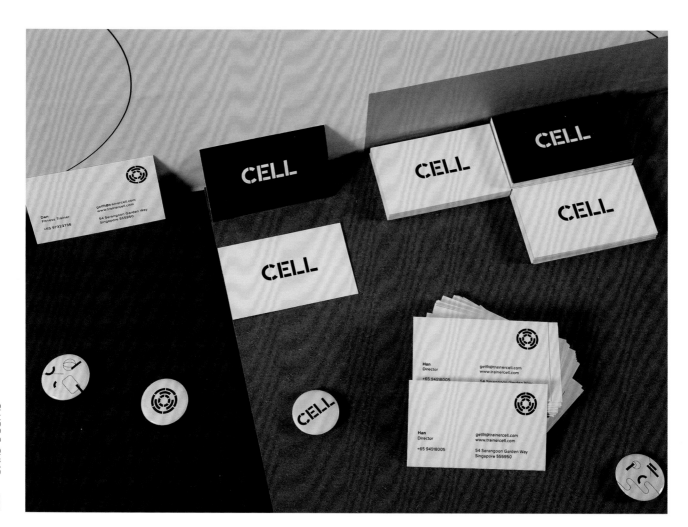

Be the best version
of yourself —
One rep at a time

@TRAINERCELL

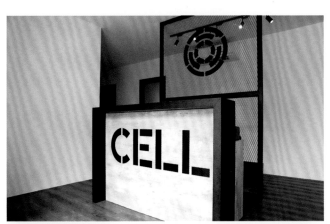

CLUBE

▸ Sports Bar

▸ DESIGN AGENCY **VOLTA Brand**
  Shaping Studio
▸ PHOTOGRAPHY **Nuno Moreira**
▸ CLIENT **CLUBE**

The rugby community in Porto, Portugal decided to open a sports bar called CLUBE. They launched the project in an old and traditional gentlemen's club and commissioned VOLTA to create their identity and decoration in a style that both fit the existing vintage style and allowed the rugby community to feel "at home." VOLTA created the tagline, the retro typography and the vintage interior decoration for the club.

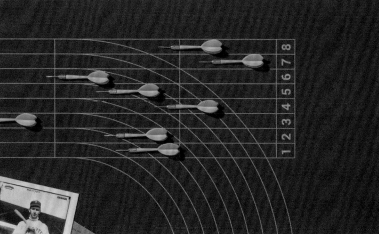

▴ "Onde se joga a 3ª Parte" in Portuguese is for "Where the third half is played."
▾ Thorough research into early- and middle-20th century sports photos was conducted and the results helped create an intricate photo mosaic on the walls.

TRAINING'S HARD?
TRY LOSING

DAVEE JONES

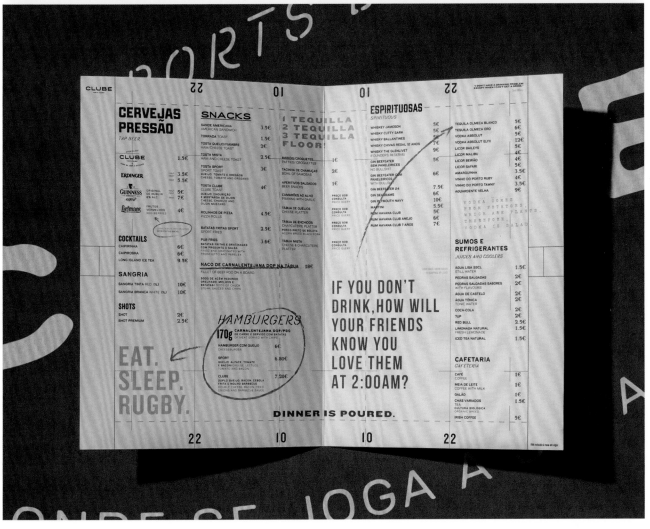

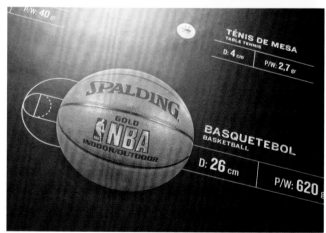

Bagheera Academy

‣ Training Center

‣ DESIGN **Tiffanie Mazellier**
‣ CLIENT **Bagheera Academy**

Bagheera Academy is a training center based on the island of New Caledonia that offers introductory courses in martial arts (capoeira, kung fu) and wants to share their philosophies. They asked Tiffanie Mazellier to create the branding to convey notions like cohesion and transcendence. The concept of this branding is based on the idea of willpower and self-elevation. The color palette chosen refers to hope and perseverance. Her goal was to put the brand in a simple and positive environment.

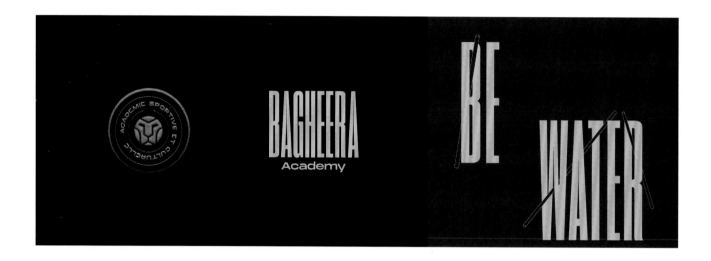

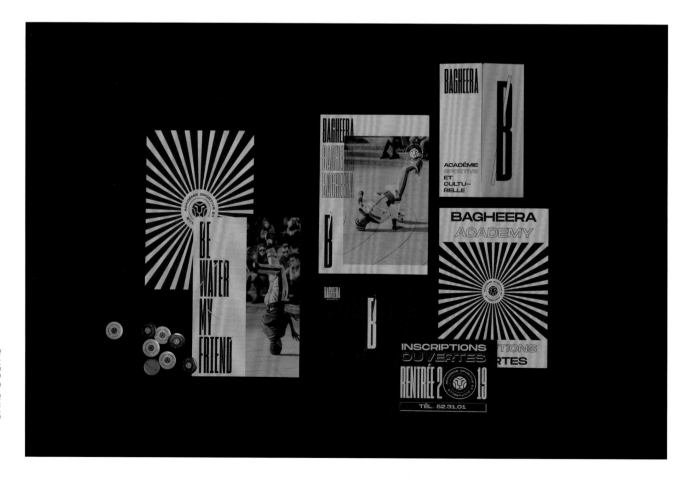

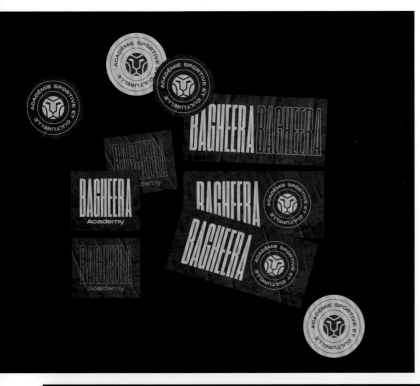

Zpin 45

▸ Cycling Club

▸ DESIGN AGENCY **Parámetro Studio**
▸ CLIENT **Zpin 45**

Zpin 45 is an indoor cycling club located in Monterrey, México. They asked Parámetro Studio for a strong identity that could speak to a young target audience. Stationary bicycles and loud music in a dark room was the experience that had to be reflected in the brand. Parámetro designed the logo based on the time span of a class—45 minutes. They modified the apex of the number four to a 45-degree angle to unveil a person going forward and the counter for the five was expanded to form the front wheel of the stationary bicycle.

Power Building

‣Fitness Studio

‣DESIGN AGENCY **9 x 9. Design**

Power Building is a fitness studio established by a group of professional fitness trainers. 9 x 9. Design got inspiration from the word "building" and built up the visual design step by step. Because the building isn't tall, the designers broke the tradition of the industrial gymnasium style and adopted a bright and simple design with a large white space, which gives the brand a sense of fashion and professionalism.

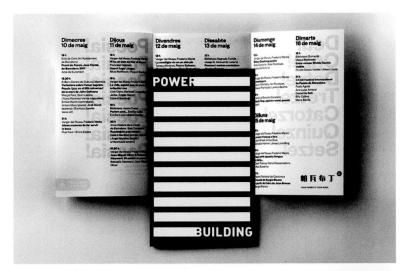

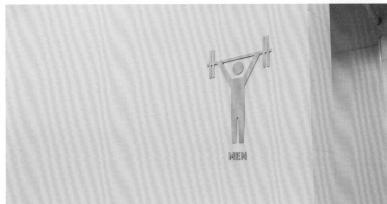

▲ Inspired by the word "building," the designers refined the form of a staircase, describing the process of building one's body day by day.

ELMNT Studio

▸Yoga & Spinning Studio

▸DESIGN AGENCY **Studio JULY**
▸DESIGN & ART DIRECTION
  Emanuel Cohen
▸PHOTOGRAPHY **Alexandre Couture,
  Kezia Nathe**

ELMNT Studio is a boutique yoga and spinning studio located in Montreal's Monkland Village. Focusing on the mind-body connection and rigorous practice and training, they offer an inner-growth and educational approach to overall fitness. Studio JULY was first commissioned to develop their visual identity, which needed to distinguish itself from the well-known "loud, bold and sweaty" fitness studios. The creative intention was to illustrate the simple principles of structure, strength, balance and rhythm using refined and technical language that would become representative of ELMNT's holistic approach to global wellness.

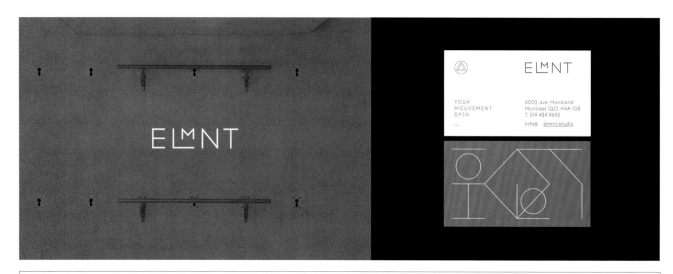

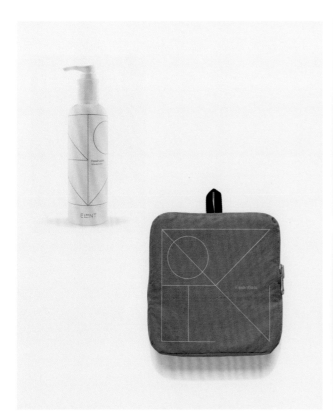

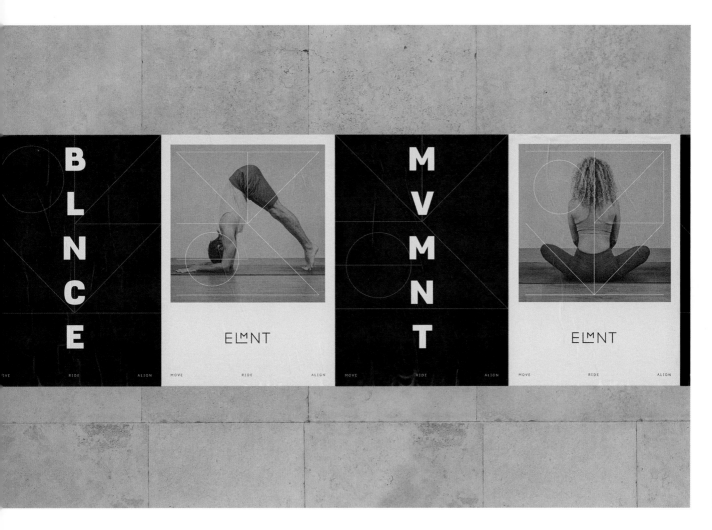

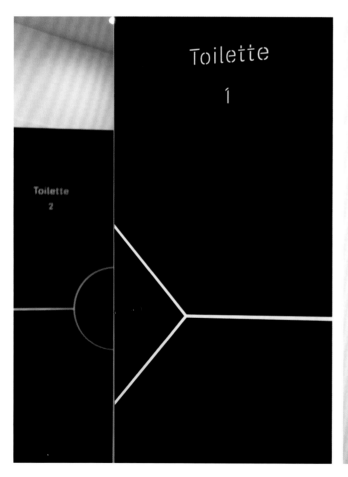

To keep our space
safe and sacred,
we have a
few requests.

ELMNT ETIQUETTE
—

**ENLEVER LES CHAUSSURES
D'EXTÉRIEUR**
Enfilez des pantoufles si vous le souhaitez.
Seulement les chaussures d'intérieur sont permises.

RESPECTER LA COMMUNAUTÉ
La communauté, c'est reconnaître que nous sommes
tous présents ensemble. N'oubliez pas de vous inscrire
à la réception.

ÊTRE PONCTUEL
Présentez-vous à l'heure ou vous risquez de
perdre votre place. Si vous avez plus de 5 minutes
de retard, vous renoncez à votre place.
Aucune exception.

*Les nouveaux cyclistes ne seront pas admis une fois le cours commencé.

SE DÉCONNECTER & ÊTRE PRÉSENT
Les téléphones cellulaires sont interdits dans les
salles de mouvement. En cas d'urgence, veuillez laisser
votre téléphone à la réception.

Si vous utilisez une montre pour suivre votre
performance, ça reste privé et non public.
Veuillez la mettre en mode silencieux et éteindre
les notifications lumineuses.

STREET SHOES OFF
Indoor shoes only. Feel free to use our slippers
at the front door.

COMMUNITY
Community starts by acknowledging we're
all here together. Please be sure to check in with
the front desk.

TIMELINESS
Show up on time or risk losing your spot.
If you're more than 5 mins late, you forfeit your
class. No exceptions.

*New riders will not be admitted after start time of class.

UNPLUG & GET PRESENT
We do not allow cell phones in the movement
studios. In case of emergency please leave your
phone with the front desk.

If you're using a watch to track your performance,
keep it personal, not public and turn off the
light and sound functions.

STAY HYDRATED
Glass bottles are fragile...

RSPCT

MOVE
RIDE
ALIGN

ELMNT

Harness Cycle

▸ Cycle Studio

▸ DESIGN AGENCY **Studio of Christine Wisnieski**
▸ DESIGN **Lauren McAndrews**
▸ CREATIVE DIRECTION **Christine Wisnieski**
▸ INTERIOR DESIGN **Danielle Deboe Harper**
▸ PHOTOGRAPHY **Suzuran, Paul Sobota**
▸ CLIENT **Harness Cycle**

When Harness Cycle began to expand, they reached out to Christine Wisnieski to refresh their brand. The studio redefined its visual aesthetic and prepared the organization for its anticipated growth. Beginning with the logo, the designers edited the existing icon to appeal to a larger audience and to perform better. They also built a family of fitness gear and products—water bottles, tote bags and clothing, and personalized the interior with custom bikes, storage racks and checkout counter.

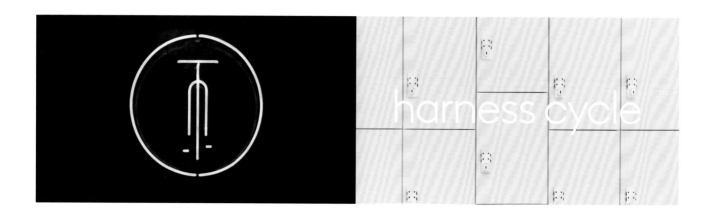

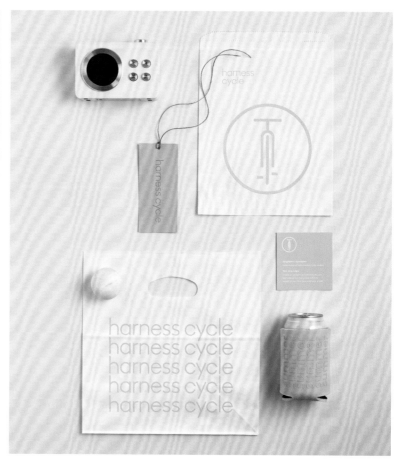

Onexing

‣ Chain Fitness Organization

‣ DESIGN AGENCY **ReflexDesign**
‣ DESIGN **Panxi**
‣ CREATIVE DIRECTION **Cai Yi**
‣ ART DIRECTION **Suning Lan**

Onexing is a chain fitness organization with eight years of history. It is known for its outstanding and professional service in bodybuilding. The client wanted to enhance consumer recognition of its core business and create an even more professional experience by refreshing the brand. Based on its core business, ReflexDesign came up with the slogan of "Onexing changes everything," which highlighted that changing the body is a persistent and gradual process. Echoing the concept of gradual change, they used a gradient font and color to design the holistic visual identity.

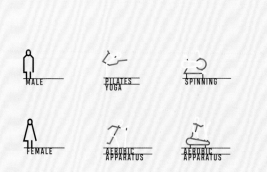

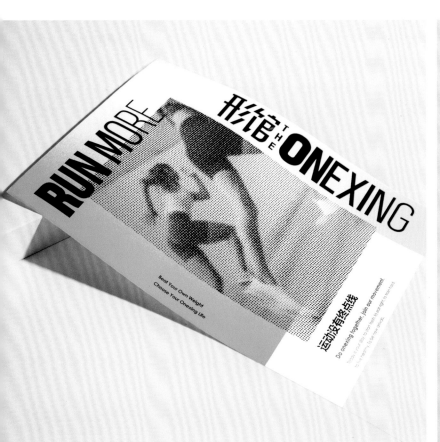

Making Waves

▸ Swimming Facility

▸ DESIGN AGENCY **Nothing Design Studio**
▸ DESIGN **Rahul Bhogal**
▸ CREATIVE DIRECTION **Rahul Bhogal**
▸ PHOTOGRAPHY **Rahul Bhogal**

After 25 years in business and with a new facility under construction, the family-owned business was looking to revitalize its brand identity. Wanting to stay true to its roots of care, passion and enthusiasm, they asked Nothing Design Studio to help design an identity that created excitement and confidence. The team redesigned their entire system to work fluidly across all communication methods, including refreshing their logo, designing custom icons and environmental design.

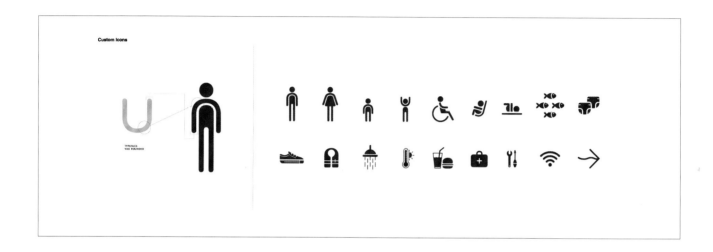

PLEASE KEEP
FOOD AND DRINKS
OUT OF PLAY AREA

CAUTION
AVOID
DEEP DIVES

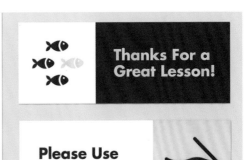

Thanks For a
Great Lesson!

CAUTION –
SLIPPERY
WHEN WET

Please Use
Other Door

Please Double Diaper

Two swim diapers with a snug fit around the legs and
waist are required for all swimmers under 36 months,
as well as older children who are not fully potty-trained.

Please help us prevent leakage into the pool,
which causes a temporary pool closure.

ALWAYS CLEAN!

Family
Change Room

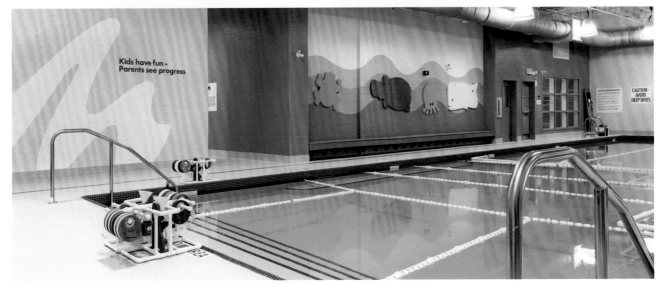

Kids have fun –
Parents see progress

b!well Wellness & Yoga

▸Yoga Studio

▸DESIGN AGENCY **papa tom**
▸DESIGN **Pascal Palmieri,**
 Thomas Korell, Catharina Demmel
▸PHOTOGRAPHY **Pascal Palmieri**
▸CLIENT **b!well Wellness & Yoga**

b!well is a yoga and wellness club. The idea behind b!well is to maintain or even improve personal well-being to become a bit happier in everyday life. The client wanted to find a name and create a logo that would provide strength and joy and serenity, while focusing on the positive. The challenge was to express the characteristics of the founder, Bibo Wacker, in addition to the club's health aspects. After experiencing their yoga classes, the designers decided the values of strength, joy and serenity should be reflected directly in the word mark, and should deliver the message. "b!well" became the motto as conveying wishes.

▾ The colorful hammocks are the main features of the studio. The design team was allowed to collect different elements and experiences from the customers thus creating a moving visual identity.

Palestra

▸ Fitness Club

▸ DESIGN AGENCY **Brandon Archibald**
▸ DESIGN **Anton Storozhev,**
  Elena Parhisenko, Yuriy Domovesov
▸ CREATIVE DIRECTION **Boris Alexandrov,**
  Anna Alexandrova

Palestra is a new premium fitness club that positions itself as a place to inspire people to live a healthy life and follow a balanced lifestyle. Brandon Archibald was commissioned to create a logo and corporate identity, interior branding and an advertising campaign for the club. The name Palestra, from the Greek word "Παλαίστρα," refers to a private gymnastics school in ancient Greece. The outcome combines the gym's Greek roots and modern sports aesthetics, which can be seen in the style elements.

HC Fitness Plaza

‣ Fitness Club

‣ DESIGN AGENCY **vegrande**®
‣ PHOTOGRAPHY **Grayscalemx**
‣ CLIENT **Mauricio Abraham**

vegrande® was commissioned to create a new concept that blended exercise, nutrition, wellness and CrossFit training, all in one place. It is the first mall in Merida, Mexico focused only on health and exercise.

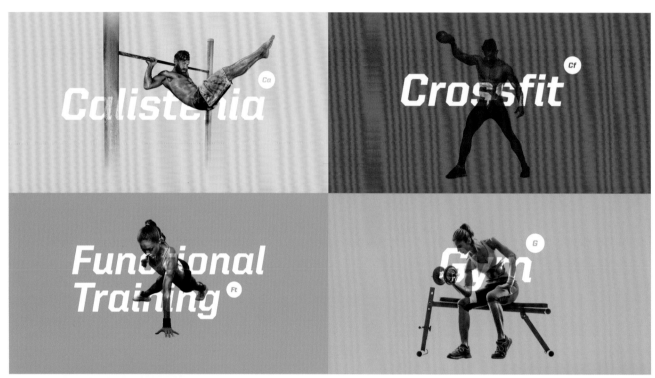

V1BE

▸ Gym

▸ DESIGN AGENCY **BGN**
▸ DESIGN **Jason Flynn**
▸ CREATIVE DIRECTION **David Newton**
▸ PROJECT MANAGEMENT **Paul Bailey**

BGN was commissioned to create an identity, a suite of materials and an online platform to launch a boutique gym brand, which aims to provide intense heart rate-monitored, high-intensity interval training or HIIT workouts. The designers highlighted the numeral "1" within the name and brand logo by using negative space to create its outline. This became a recognizable hero marquee used across all materials. The color palette was stripped-back and predominantly utilized black and white to keep the brand foundations strong and some bright colors were used to represent the vibrant and energetic nature of both the V1BE studio environment and the classes they offer.

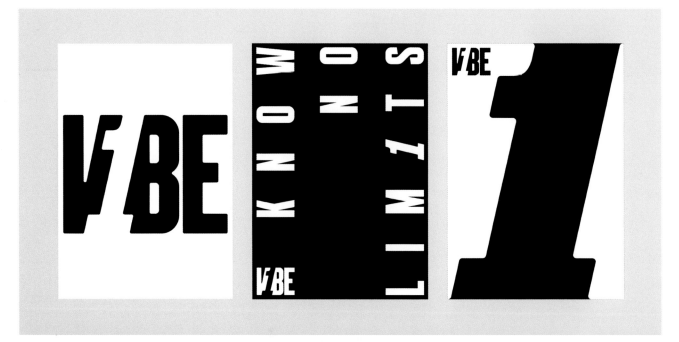

Ground Zero

‣ Spinning & Boxing Studio

‣ DESIGN AGENCY **Bravo**
‣ DESIGN **Shermaine Wee**
‣ CREATIVE DIRECTION **Edwin Tan**
‣ PROJECT MANAGEMENT **Carisia Chew**
‣ SPACE DESIGN **Eightytwo**

Ground Zero is a spinning and boxing studio that pushes one's limits through immersive, high-energy experiences filled with light and sound. Bravo conceived of a place where the rhythm of the music builds boxers' energy, while the dark space, raw concrete and neon lights exude dystopian vibes that awaken your survival instincts.

Kristallijn

▸ Ice Skating Rink

▸ DESIGN AGENCY **Studio WillemsPeeters**

Kristallijn, based in Ghent, is the biggest ice rink in Belgium. Henk Willems and Jelena Peeters were tasked with creating a new identity that was an evolution of the current brand, but was redesigned to better express the vibrant energy of the ice rink. For Kristallijn, they created "More Than Ice," meaning it is not only a space for all levels of ice sports, but a public space for relaxing, socializing, enjoying, discovering and celebrating. The new brand is expressive, fun, spontaneous, and strives and stretches across any platform of communication.

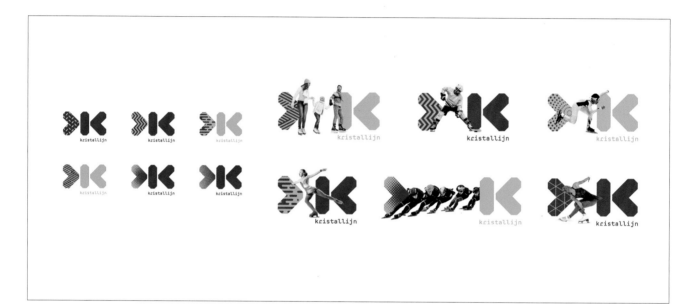

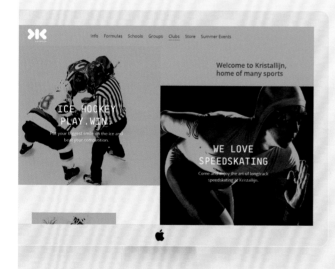

Scottish Swimming

▸ Sporting Organization

▸ DESIGN AGENCY **Touch**
▸ PHOTOGRAPHY **Al Ferrier**
▸ CLIENT **Scottish Swimming**

Scottish Swimming, the national governing body for swimming in Scotland, appointed Touch to create a brand-new identity system that would work across a range of applications, from national event signage to swimming certificates. As the organization works across all levels of the sport in Scotland, from teaching infants basic water confidence to training world-class elite athletes, the new identity had to be equally broad-ranging and adaptable, on top of being instantly recognizable when surrounded by the identities for similar organizations. Since the rebrand and launch, Touch has continued to work with Scottish Swimming, creating the branding for major championship events and campaigns to promote aquatic sports for health.

Le Ballon

▸ Football Club

▸ DESIGN AGENCY **Yorgo&Co.**
▸ PHOTOGRAPHY **Louis David Najar, Emmanuelle Lubaki**
▸ CLIENT **Le Ballon FC**

A group of Parisian friends created Le Ballon, a hip and friendly venue to watch the 2014 FIFA World Cup. This project soon outlived the sporting event and continues to grow, with events worldwide and a clothing label.

Aqua Sports & Spa

‣ Sports Club

‣ DESIGN AGENCY **artless Inc.**
‣ DESIGN **Shun Kawakami, Nao Nozawa**
‣ CREATIVE & ART DIRECTION
  Shun Kawakami
‣ LOGO DESIGN **Leonie Aiko**
‣ CLIENT **The Sports Connection Inc.**

artless Inc. was put in charge of branding and design consultation for Aqua Sports & Spa, a members-only sports club that re-opened in June 2016 after renovation. The club provides fitness, recreation, café, and relaxation. As their facility was undergoing renovation, the brand also was revamped, including renaming and redesigning the logo and visual identity. artless Inc. was engaged to take part in branding and design consultation. What they aimed to achieve with the project was to create a balance of sophistication and minimalism with the belief that it would appeal to a wide audience.

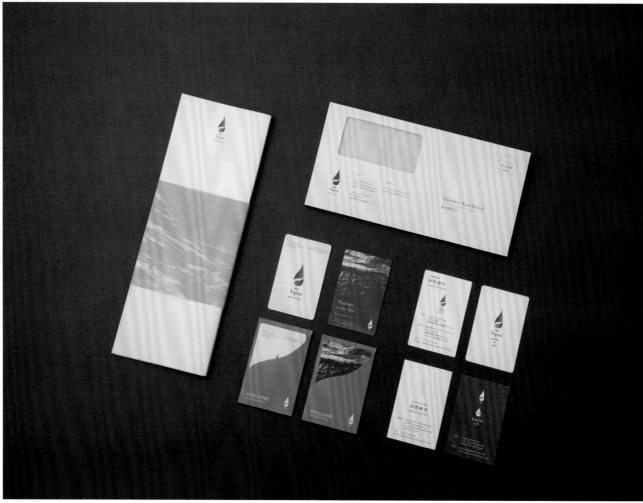

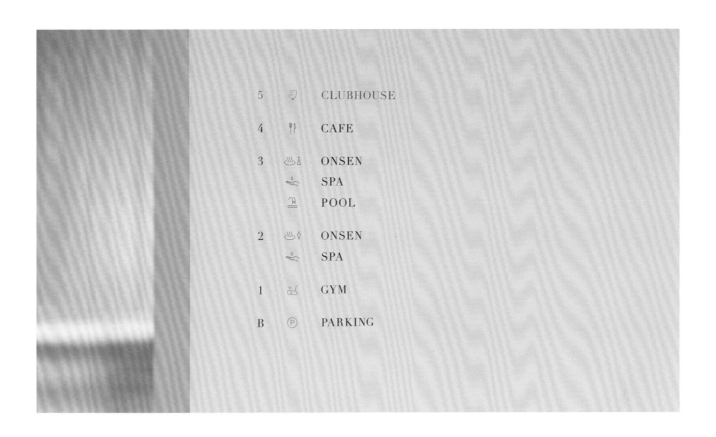

5   🛡   CLUBHOUSE

4   🍴   CAFE

3   ♨   ONSEN

      🍵   SPA

      〰   POOL

2   ♨   ONSEN

      🍵   SPA

1   🚴   GYM

B   Ⓟ   PARKING

Fitness Yoga Club

▸ Fitness Center & Yoga Club

▸ DESIGN AGENCY **Ehrhorn Hummerston**

The client wanted to introduce a new category to the fitness market—a high-end, exclusive club. The client was responsible for buying the right equipment and hiring the right staff. Ehrhorn Hummerston was hired to develop an exclusive design to realize the intention. They developed and designed the brand in all aspects: the logo, website, photos, film for website and social media, infographics, brochures, posters, ads and all communications.

WIT Fitness

‣ Gym

‣ DESIGN AGENCY **FLUORO.**

Founded in 2015, WIT Fitness grew quickly. They came to FLUORO. with a bold vision—"create a brand identity, digital strategy and design language that would assist in forging their position as the world's leading training hub specialist." FLUORO. created a graphic system that uses typographic messaging, grids and patterns that reflect the brand's urban appeal and city influence. This created a contemporary, fresh and bold aesthetic conveying movement and athleticism. They developed and implemented this design strategy across all parts of the user journey—WIT retail and training websites, social channels and in-store digital systems—an ecosystem designed to showcase the entire portfolio of retail brands, stores and services.

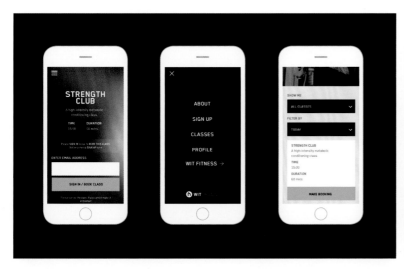

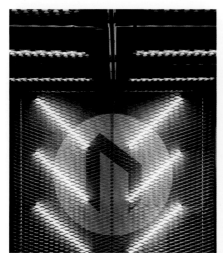

Bounce Ping Pong

▸ Social Ping Pong Club

▸ DESIGN AGENCY **Ascend Studio**
▸ DESIGN **Yarron Frauenfelder**
▸ CREATIVE DIRECTION **Paul Croxton**

Ascend Studio was commissioned to establish Bounce Ping Pong as an original, authentic, fun and premium social entertainment offering. Their rebranding includes repositioning, values, brand proposition, tone of voice and full brand guidelines. The activation materials included logo design, an identity system, advertising, posters, signage, menus, uniforms, stationery, website and social media assets.

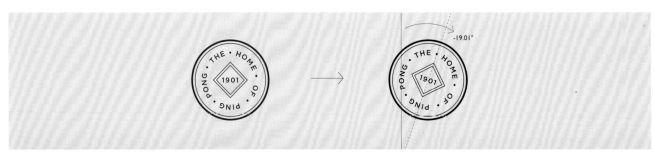

Sen Flow

‣ Fitness & Wellness Studio

‣ DESIGN **Belen Ramos, Jason Cooper**
‣ CLIENT **Cathy Pham**

Sen Flow is a fitness and wellness studio based in the heart of Sydney's Vietnamese community. The brand audience is predominantly female and Vietnamese, so the outcome needed to stay true to its community and values, but entice new customers to "Join the Flow" by standing out among the competition. The name was derived from "sen" meaning "lotus" and "purity of mind" in Vietnamese. "Flow" is for energy and water flow. Sen Flow is energetic and calm at the same time.

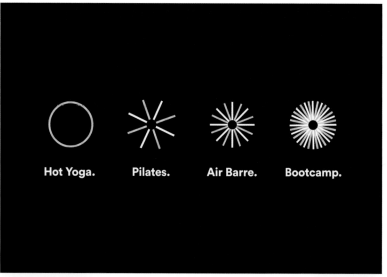
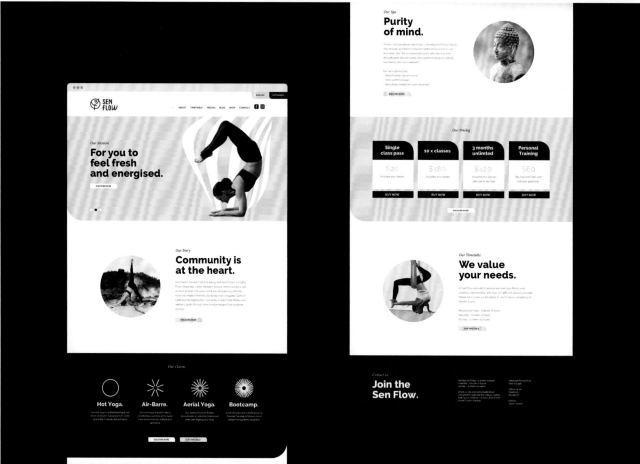

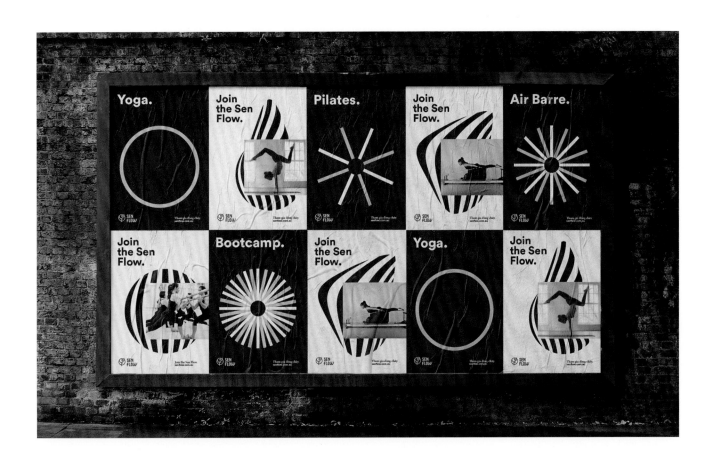

Here.

‣ Wellbeing Studio

‣ DESIGN AGENCY **ED.**
‣ DESIGN **Cam Tidy, Elliot Schultz**

The wellbeing studio, Here., needed a name, brand and website to introduce themselves to the world. ED. began with a name that summarizes what the brand stands for and the simple, friendly logotype introduces the importance of mindfulness. The calming, monochromatic color palette discreetly applied urges focus while the resulting "pill press" effect of the typography speaks to the evidence-based practice.

KOR

▸ Fitness Club

▸ DESIGN AGENCY **StudioDBD**

KOR wanted a complete identity and naming for a new fitness experience opening in central Manchester, England. They wanted something a little different. StudioDBD came up with the name KOR, a unit of measurement, because fitness is often measured in small details. They also created a bold and graphic visual language for KOR, featuring type, imagery and iconography.

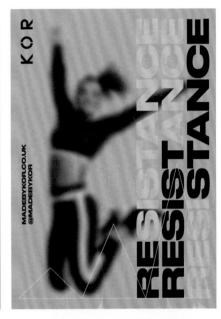

VAUNCE

‣ Trampoline Park

‣ DESIGN AGENCY **Plus X**
‣ CREATIVE DIRECTION **Myungsup Shin**

VAUNCE Trampoline Park was a brand-new play and cultural space. People enjoy sports to experience freedom and get a sense of release, and Plus X wanted to express its own brand identity using a defined design principle based on its own philosophy. VAUNCE defined five core values—health, enjoyment, freedom, achievement and culture—for its brand to encompass a passion for freedom with healthy enjoyment. Based on them, Plus X developed design keywords and achieved consistent communication at the brand's user interface.

LaLiga

‣ Football League

‣ DESIGN AGENCY **IS Creative Studio.**
‣ DESIGN **Rommina Dolorier, Maria Boada,
  Alessandra Casanova, Alexa Tang**
‣ CREATIVE DIRECTION **Richars Meza**

A huge challenge filled IS Creative Studio. with excitement to work with the best football league in the world. Their goal was to design a contemporary evolution towards a strong, vibrant and dynamic identity that expresses the values of unity and team spirit. They constructed the symbol and the ball, accentuating the shapes with rounded angles to give the brand a more friendly, warm and human approach. Also, they defined the typefaces and the right proportions of the new system for the various applications of the brand.

SATS

▸ Fitness Club

▸ DESIGN AGENCY **Bold Scandinavia**
▸ DESIGN **Bendik Høibraaten,
 Derek Ercolano**
▸ CREATIVE DIRECTION **Roar Sager**
▸ TYPE DESIGN **Letters from Sweden**
▸ PHOTOGRAPHY **Simon Skreddernes**

SATS is the biggest chain of fitness clubs in the Nordic countries. Bold Scandinavia was asked to redesign and re-position SATS and Elixia as one brand with a premium and Nordic feel. The identity concept is based on visualizing the movement and energy of training through the dynamic typography, the brand images and user experience. The photography captures the movements and the precise moment. Slanted letters create a unique typeface that constantly moves. The juxtaposition of the type and actions of training create momentum within the brand identity. The color palette evokes a premium feel with its predominantly dark blue hues and coral highlights.

Forma & Saúde

▸ Pilates Studio

▸ DESIGN **Ramona Katcheika Paloschi**

Forma & Saúde is a studio that offers Pilates classes, physiotherapy and global postural re-education (GPR). The aims were to re-establish a close sentiment with the company's activities through a realistic, relevant and recognizable identity that would be easily adaptable to several types of media used in the sector. The designer used the "&" joining the words "forma" and "saúde" to create a brand identity, hinting at Pilates movements with an exercise ball. A fresh color palette promotes energy and enthusiasm, and a dark shade was chosen to give people a sense of trust and security.

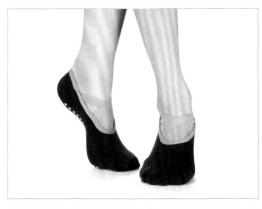

ProPulsion

▸ Workout App

▸ DESIGN AGENCY **hatem + d**

hatem + d was commissioned to create a new brand identity for ProPulsion, a personalized training service offering sport and nutritional coaching via a mobile app. The first part of the project was to create a short name that would position the brand as a digital fitness coach. Perpetual undulation of training cycles inspired the creative team to develop a strong brand identity.

Nike Golf Club

▸ Golf Club

▸ DESIGN AGENCY **Mother Design**
▸ DESIGN **Christian Cervantes, Thomas Humeau, George Lavender, Dan Broadwood, Cat Cooke, Mark Aver**

A new generation of golfers who love golf, but not traditional golf clubs is emerging. Nike asked Mother Design to help design a modern golf club to attract and serve them. Nike Golf Club is a premium, member-based program that gives modern golfers access to the best of Nike Golf— everything from exclusive content like pro tips to first dibs on limited-edition apparel. Traditional golf clubs are seen as conservative, conformist and homogenous. But this generation is the opposite—forward-thinking, creative, multi-dimensional and dynamic. Mother Design set out to create an identity that reflected the spirit of this new generation of golfers while, at the same time, honoring the sport.

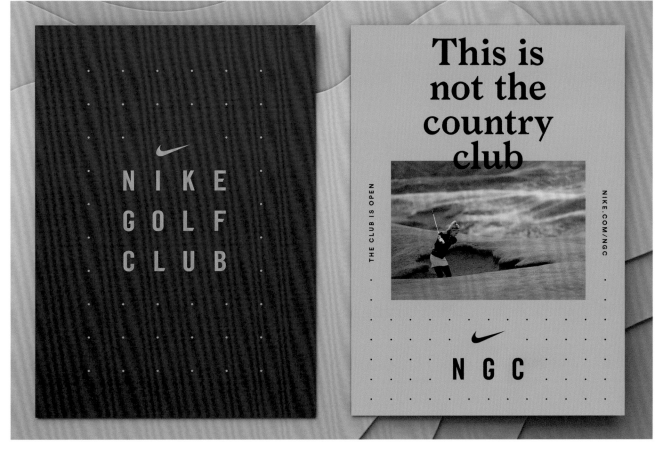

The DFB Rebranding

‣ Football Association

‣ DESIGN AGENCY **Strichpunkt Design**
‣ CREATIVE DIRECTION **Ulla Oberdörffer**
‣ ART DIRECTION **Christine Wolf,**
  Stephanie Zehender, Leon Thau
‣ DESIGN **Orson Podgorski**
‣ PROJECT DESIGN **Raphael Knolmayer,**
  Leon Bauer
‣ CLIENT **Deutscher Fussball-Bund,**
  Juri Müller, Ralf Koch

The desire of the Deutscher Fußball-Bund (DFB) to strengthen the overall brand was focused on allowing the sub-brands to make a noticeable contribution to the umbrella brand without losing their characteristic diversity. Based on the principle of modular design, the relevant design elements were further developed across all brands and adapted to the sub-brands.

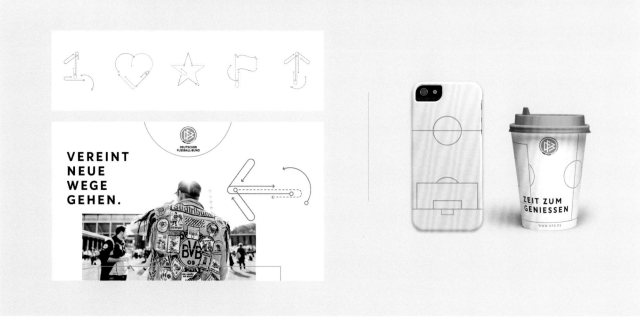

DFB SANS BOLD

Aa

DFB SANS REGULAR

Saisonstart 2019

ABCDEFGHIJKLMNOPQRSTUVWXYZ
abcdefghijklmnopqrstuvwxyz ?!,;%$@
123456789 0

DFB SANS ITALIC

Saisonstart 2019

ABCDEFGHIJKLMNOPQRSTUVWXYZ
abcdefghijklmnopqrstuvwxyz ?!,;%$@
123456789 0

DFB SANS CONDENSED

Saisonstart 2019

ABCDEFGHIJKLMNOPQRSTUVWXYZ
abcdefghijklmnopqrstuvwxyz ?!,;%$@
123456789 0

DFB STENCIL

ABCDEFGHIJKLM
→ ↗ &2019*

LOGO

ICONS

WIR MACHEN

HELDEN

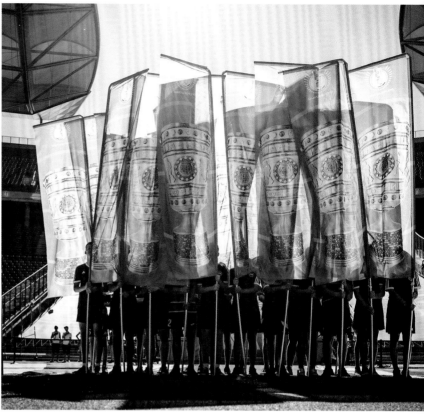

WIR
LEBEN
FÜR
DEN
FUSSBALL

DIE MANNSCHAFT

La Montgolfière

‣ Social Sports Club

‣ DESIGN AGENCY **Brand Brothers**
‣ CREATIVE DIRECTION **Johan Debit**
‣ CLIENT **La Montgolfière**

La Montgolfière, built in the 1850s and formerly used as a hot air balloon canvas factory, is a social sports club located near the Canal Saint-Martin in Paris. More than a simple fitness center, it is a fusion among several atmospheres (music, art, sport, food). Brand Brothers was tasked to create a brand identity, a graphic territory and various printed materials for the club. The requirement was to give the place a memorable visual identity with impeccable graphic work, while injecting a dose of extravagance and roughness. Brand Brothers oriented their work around two main axes: rigor of design and freedom of tone. They created a simple graphic system, based on the Panamera font and fir green, the initial hue of the beams forming the framework of the façade.

▾ For pre-opening, Brand Brothers developed a visual language based on multiple typographical and photographic compositions and strong verbal hooks.

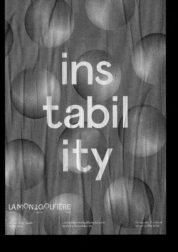

EVENTS
&TEAMS

Jelena Peeters

*"It was for me the combination of being
an Olympic athlete on the one hand
and being a designer on the other hand."*

Jelena Peeters is a former long-track speed skater from Antwerp, Belgium. In 2014, Jelena participated in her first Olympic Games in Sochi. At her second Winter Games in PyeongChang, she took 10th place in the 5,000 meter speed skating competition. Jelena holds a master's degree in graphic design from the Royal Academy of Fine Arts in Antwerp. She has worked as a designer at Edhv and Studio Kluif where she won a silver European design award.

1. How did your experience as a speed skater influence your design?

As a 9-year-old child, I started roller skating. So, I have seen and used lots of sportswear since then. And as a 16-year-old, I made my first designs for the local skating club. This must have had its influence. In this particular design project, the Winter Olympics 2018 speed skating outfit and RBSF rebranding, it was, for me, the combination of being an Olympic athlete on the one hand and being a designer on the other hand. It turned out that both jobs complemented each other really well in this job.

2. What are the basic steps you would take to start a sports graphic design project?

As in any project, it is about finding ways to express what you want to tell. It is a search for ideas, you come to a stream of inspiration and you start making designs. In this case, we wanted to express passion, movement and guts. My collaborator, Henk Willems, and I started this project by viewing all the craziest sports suits ever.

3. How did you get ideas for the RBSF rebranding project and the Winter Olympics 2018 speed skating outfit design?

The idea grew from the letter "B" of Belgium. We started with a logo. We wanted it distinctly strong, proud, fast and, of course, to have a Belgian touch. We arrived at an angular B, which was the start of everything. We made patterns that were combined in the logo. These logo variants were brought together in a new pattern. We passed this project on to each other several times and worked on each other's designs. In this way, you always take steps that you would not immediately expect. This worked very smoothly and inspiringly for us.

4. Did you have a big team for the RBSF rebranding and Winter Olympics 2018 speed skating outfit project?

Henk and I collaborated with the Belgian Speed Skating Federation and with the clothing manufacturer, AGU. The collaboration with the clothing manufacturer was not easy. We received little technical support, so, eventually, we had to use paper to cut out the patterns and imagine what the design would do in 3D. Also, the color yellow was not bright enough on the fabric. Fortunately, the lighting on the Olympic ice rink was so bright that the yellow turned out very nice.

5. The outfit design is just one part of the broader Olympic Games design. What advantages and limits did you meet when you were designing for such a global and prestigious design project?

The fabric of the skate suits is really difficult to print and it was, therefore, only possible to print certain parts of the suit. It is a difficult fabric that should, of course, be aerodynamic in the first place. The short-track speed skating suits had an additional obligation, namely that the flag of the country needed to be printed large on the chest. Of course, we were limited to the Belgian colors, but, otherwise, we got freedom. There is a lot of global interest in the Olympic Games. So, we seized the opportunity and made a suit that is special and striking and shows guts.

6. You made many posters for speed skating games held around the world and they were more or less integrated into the local culture. How did you do that?

I already held a master's degree in graphic design before I started a professional skating career. One day, I got injured and I was forced to take a rest. Because of this, I took my pencil and started working on a poster series. It would be one poster per tournament. We traveled continuously from tournament to tournament. Together with my coach, we were always thinking about what the next poster could be. It was especially fun and relaxing to do this during the many hours of rest in between training sessions and during the long travels. Of course, there was a lot of looking around and inspiration was gained by the traveling itself.

7. What's the main difference between Olympic design and other sports-themed commercial projects?

The enormous interest of the audience is exceptional. It is an honor to be allowed to design for such an event. At this very moment, we're working on the design of all sportswear for the Belgian athletes for Tokyo 2020. I think designing for the Olympics is very addictive.

RBSF Rebranding and Winter Olympics 2018
Speed Skating Outfit

‣ Speed Skating Organization & Team

‣ DESIGN AGENCY **Studio WillemsPeeters**
‣ DESIGN **Jelena Peeters, Henk Willems**
‣ PHOTOGRAPHY **Lieven Dirckx**
‣ CLIENT **Royal Belgian Speed Skating Federation**

The Royal Belgian Speed Skating Federation (RBSF) asked Jelena Peeters and Henk Willems to update their visual identity and to create a strong, dynamic and future-proof sports brand. They wanted to create more awareness for the sport and attract new athletes and fans. After the designers developed a new brand platform "passion into motion," they were commissioned to further create an identity system that could work across all touchpoints. The design for the skating outfit for the Winter Olympics 2018 in PyeongChang put the finishing touch on the rebranding of the RBSF.

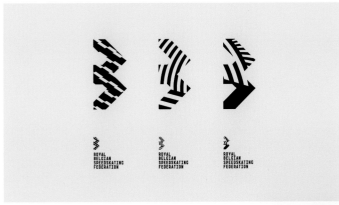

The Nike South Africa Team

▸ Team

▸ DESIGN AGENCY **Futura**
▸ OTHER CONTRIBUTORS **The Kinetic Studio, Daniel Ting Chong**
▸ PHOTOGRAPHY **Antonia Steyn, Justin Dingwall**

Futura was asked to develop a team identity that could be used internally within the new Nike South Africa offices, team events, presentations and other occasions. They used the team's maxims to create a typographic identity that drew inspiration from the informal type work found in and around Johannesburg.

Reebok Running Squad

▸Runners Club

▸DESIGN AGENCY **Animal**
▸CREATIVE DIRECTION **Kunel Gaur,
Sharon Borgoyary**
▸ART DIRECTION **Sugandha Kharya,
Pranay Patwardhan**
▸CLIENT **Reebok**

Reebok Running Squad, owned and operated by Reebok, approached Animal with the intent of changing their visual identity and the way they speak to their target audience for their on-ground training and professional running workshops. Animal proceeded to create an identity that reflects the younger mindset and speaks directly to the serious runner. They created the identity based on the concept that running takes one to a place beyond one's surroundings and into a zone of one's own, a trance where it is just the person and the track. It is personal, it is precious, it is off-limits to others and it is a time when people are in their own zone.

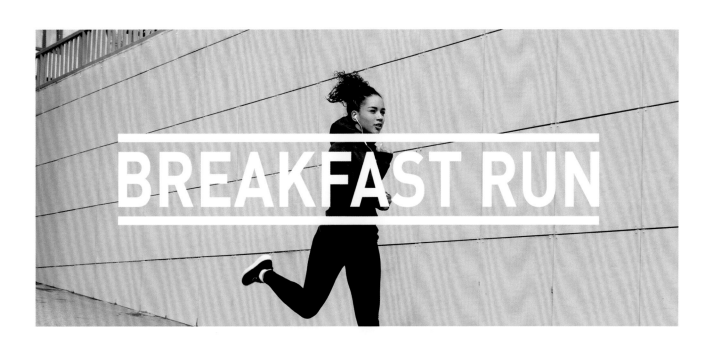

BREAKFAST RUN

OWN YOUR ZONE
DELHI

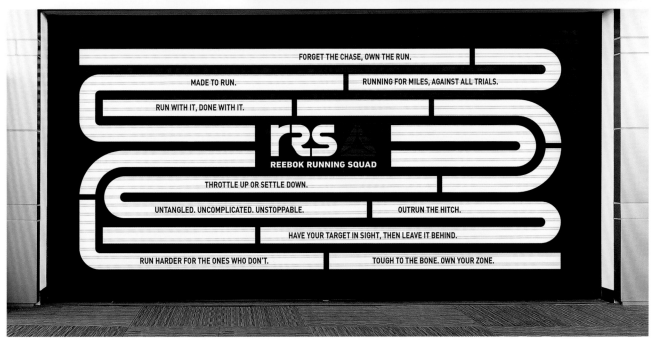

FORGET THE CHASE, OWN THE RUN.

MADE TO RUN.

RUNNING FOR MILES, AGAINST ALL TRIALS.

RUN WITH IT, DONE WITH IT.

r͜͜s
REEBOK RUNNING SQUAD

THROTTLE UP OR SETTLE DOWN.

UNTANGLED. UNCOMPLICATED. UNSTOPPABLE.

OUTRUN THE HITCH.

HAVE YOUR TARGET IN SIGHT, THEN LEAVE IT BEHIND.

RUN HARDER FOR THE ONES WHO DON'T.

TOUGH TO THE BONE. OWN YOUR ZONE.

Czech Ice Hockey Rebranding

‣ Ice Hockey Organization

‣ DESIGN AGENCY **Go4Gold**
‣ ART DIRECTION **Alan Záruba**
‣ LOGO DESIGN **Go4Gold, Tomáš Vachuda**
‣ TYPE DESIGN **Tomáš Brousil**
‣ CLIENT **Czech Ice Hockey Association**

The Czech Ice Hockey Association is a civil society organization, a national governing body of ice hockey in the Czech Republic and one of the founding members of the International Ice Hockey Federation, which began in 1908. Go4Gold were asked to design a new visual identity for the Czech Ice Hockey Association, including its new name and logo. The new logo included a stylized lion head, a new overall visual style and a custom typeface called Hokejista. Apart from that, they also designed further brands for the national team as well as other sub-projects.

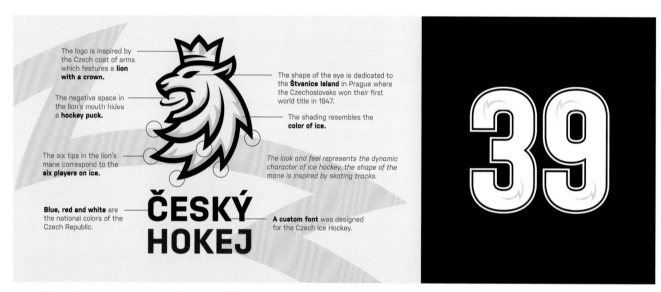

XVIth All-Sokol Slet 2018

‣ Sporting Event

‣ DESIGN AGENCY **Studio Najbrt**
‣ ART DIRECTION **Aleš Najbrt,
  Bohumil Vašák**
‣ COOPERATION **Michal Nanoru**
‣ AUTHOR **Jakub Spurný**
‣ CLIENT **Česká obec sokolská**

"Slet" is a massive gathering and theatrical performance held every six years by the Sokol movement, a gymnastics organization, and is intended to provide physical, moral and intellectual training for the nation. Its identity was often designed by the prominent artists of its day. Studio Najbrt was commissioned to create the identity for the event in 2018. They decided to base the design of the official poster for the 16th "slet" on the diagrams that use dots, lines and arrows to guide the gymnasts. The simple graphic depictions of complex choreographies reminded people of the elegant visual language of Bauhaus or the legendary Czech designer Ladislav Sutnar.

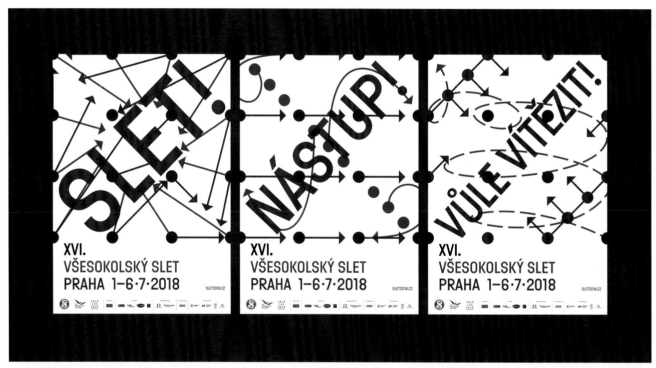

Le Quartier

▸ Basketball Event

▸ DESIGN AGENCY **Irradié**
▸ ART DIRECTION **Daniel Whiteneck**
▸ CLIENT **Nike**

To celebrate the new NBA season and the arrival of Kobe Bryant in Paris, Nike Europe launched the event "Le Quartier" in the 19th district of Paris at the Jean Jaurés gym. They commissioned Paris-based studio, Irradié, to create artworks for the event. The studio created stand-alone graphics inspired by basketball using the red and blue color palette. Their work was used in the poster mash-up covering the walls of the basketball court and was printed on shirts and tote bags.

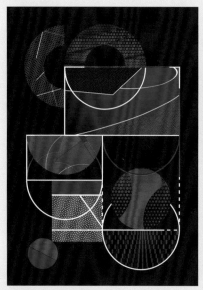

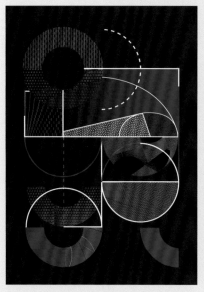

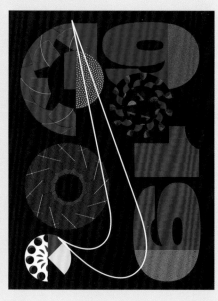

LOSC

▸ Football Team

▸ DESIGN AGENCY **Dragon Rouge**
▸ CLIENT **LOSC**

LOSC, Lille's legendary football club, commissioned Dragon Rouge to create a stronger, sportier and more modern identity. Dragon Rouge built a strong brand association between each communication element of the identity. The graphic system, illustrative forms and typography were designed from the new logo and particularly its external angles. Other tasks included the redesign of key locations (press rooms, players' changing rooms), several merchandising items and the communication campaign #FollowTheDogue.

Beach Soccer Czech Republic

‣ Beach Soccer Team

‣ DESIGN AGENCY **Code Switch**
‣ ART DIRECTION **Jan Šabach**
‣ CLIENT **Beach Soccer Czech Republic**

Beach Soccer Czech Republic approached Code Switch with a logo and identity assignment. Jan Šabach, the designer, decided to stay away from the overused motifs of palm trees, sun, ocean or a silhouette of a beach soccer player doing the signature bicycle kick because they were not persuasive for Czechs who live in a landlocked country. She created a playful logo and identity based on a custom typeface. When the logo moves, the "R" rolls over to kick the "O" and turns the letters into a player kicking a ball. The color palette was taken from the country's flag.

Alouettes de Montréal

▸Football Team

▸DESIGN AGENCY **GRDN**
▸SPECIAL COLLABORATOR **Vice Media**
▸DIRECTOR **Matt Charland**
▸VIDEOGRAPHY **Pierre-Marc Lachaine Spenard-Ko**
▸PRODUCTION **L'Éloi**
▸STYLING **Teamm**
▸MOTION DESIGN **Studio Nord Est**
▸WEB DEVELOPMENT **Bulldozer**
▸PHOTOGRAPHY **LM Chabot, Celia**

The Alouettes and the city of Montréal ties run deep. They sure both shared a lot of history since the club was founded in 1946 winning seven grey cups throughout the years. In 2017, under new management, the team rise from its heritage to begin a new chapter in its history and propel itself forward. GRDN's challenge was to rebuild the brand's inner culture while empowering its people, use it as a foundation for the rebranding and create new ways to engage the fans and the city of Montréal.

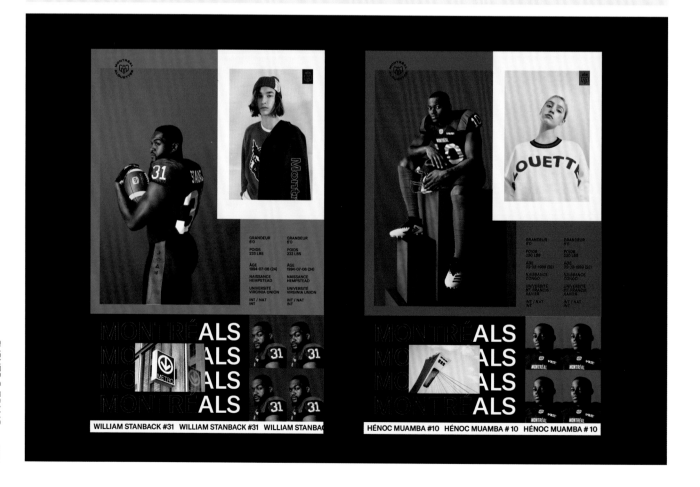

2018 London Marathon – Everybody's Race

▸ Sporting Event

▸ DESIGN AGENCY **VMLY&R**
▸ CREATIVE DIRECTION **Silmo Bonomi, Gabriel Jardim, Guto Monteiro**
▸ ART DIRECTION **Jesse Echevarria, Gabriel Jardim**
▸ MANAGING DIRECTION **Craig Elimeliah**
▸ CREATIVE TECHNOLOGY **Craig Elimeliah**
▸ CLIENT **New Balance**

New Balance was the official clothing and footwear partner of the Virgin Money London Marathon in 2018. As the global lead creative agency for New Balance, VMLY&R designed for the event. Marathon runners need more than just their shoes. They need to know they are not in this alone and that there is a whole community of people supporting them as they embark on this journey. New Balance used this spirit and turned the London Marathon into a bold declaration of solidarity—one where every runner's individual purpose was joined with the grand purpose to move the world forward, showing everyone they are all in this together.

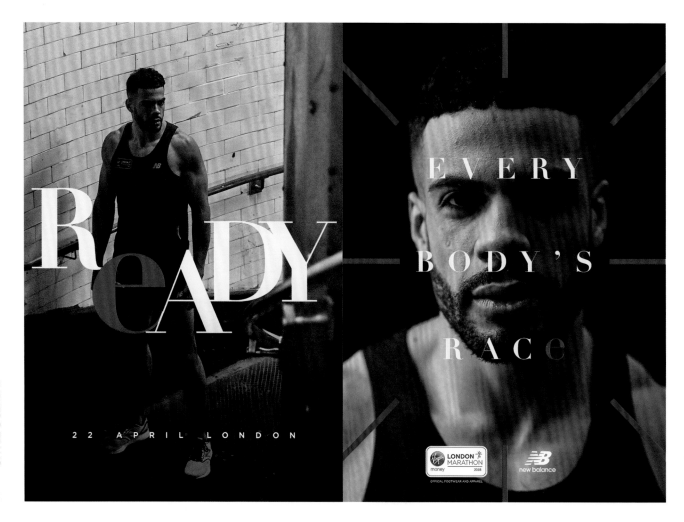

WYŚCIG

▸ Road Bicycle Racing

▸ DESIGN AGENCY **Blürb Studio**
▸ PHOTOGRAPHY **Mateusz Wojnar, Szymon Gruchalski**

WYŚCIG is a bicycle race held annually in Poland. Combined with a fundraiser, it is organized as a closing celebration of the cycling season and a summary of all the cycling tours, races and experiences throughout the past months. Blürb Studio designed complete branding materials, including posters, advertising banners, car advertisements, press materials, web content, cycling equipment, invitations and flags. The design process was based on the idea that the visual identity needed to be gripping, inviting, engaging, mobilizing, lively, dynamic and lightweight.

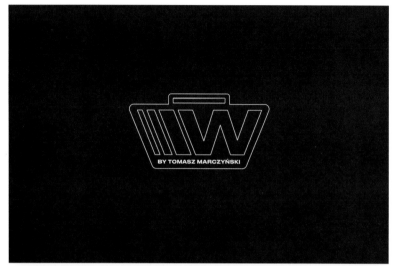

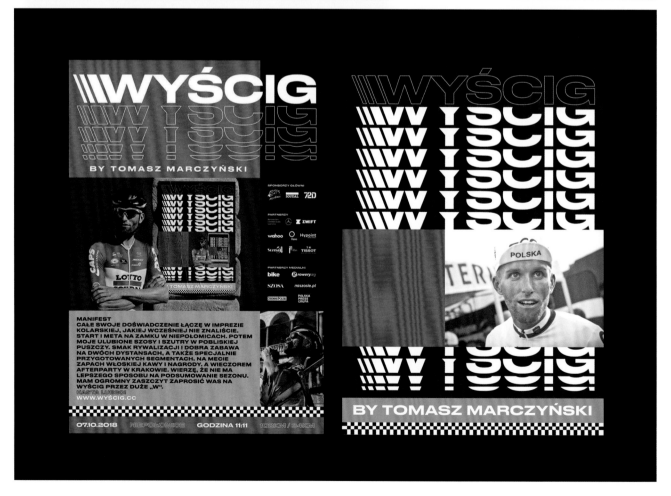

EpiqE

▸ Horse Racing Brand & Competition

▸ DESIGN AGENCY **Dragon Rouge**
▸ PHOTOGRAPHY **Alexis Cottin, Scoopdyga**
▸ CLIENT **PMU**

The French horse-racing industry wanted to return horse racing to the hearts of the French population. Dragon Rouge was asked to create a new brand that would unite the public and offer a unique experience in horse racing. To communicate the vision of the project, they invented the brand EpiqE. Inspired by the jockey silks, which are specific to the universe of horse racing, EpiqE brought horse-racing culture to life with an identity that combines appearance and stature. Dragon Rouge also did branding for the horse-racing competition.

Hackney Half

‣ Sporting Event

‣ DESIGN AGENCY **Soft Power**
‣ CREATIVE DIRECTION **Adriano Furtardo, Jonathan Seary**
‣ PHOTOGRAPHY **Alina Negoita**

The Hackney Half Marathon in London is regularly ranked as one of the top half marathons in the United Kingdom. The 2019 race was the first to partner with Nike London. Soft Power was commissioned to create a timeless identity that could act as a structure for each year's creative collaborators to bring their own twists to the Hackney Half. Their strategy was to create a brand that was a celebration of running's ability to build communities. The "H" logo represents multiple runners moving together on parallel paths, while the oblique angle adds perspective and depth to represent distance. The spine of the brand is underpinned by the H grid system, which brings uniformity to all applications.

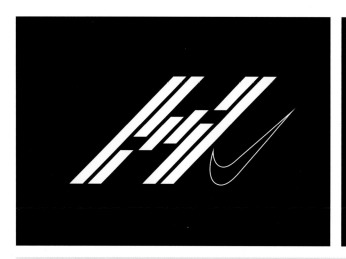
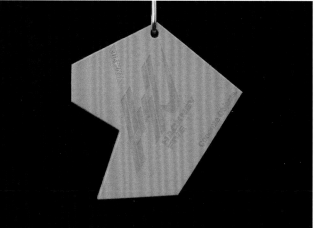

Intecracy Open

▸ Sporting Event

▸ DESIGN **Dima Goreniuk**
▸ CLIENT **Intecracy Open**

The Intecracy Open is a tennis tournament. Dima Goreniuk was commissioned to design a visual identity, including web and type design, for the event. The visual system consists of multiple layers. The logo always includes the graphic of tennis balls, but the symbol inside is variable. First, it was a palm tree, but it will change with the host city. The other parts of the identity are taken from the game itself and are treated in a playful way.

Peak Running Campaign

▸ Sporting Event

▸ DESIGN **Mane Tatoulian**
▸ CREATIVE DIRECTION **Peak design team, Mane Tatoulian**
▸ PHOTOGRAPHY **Peak**
▸ CLIENT **Peak**

Peak is an innovative company based in China. They design, manufacture and distribute sports products, including footwear, clothing and accessories. Peak's philosophy is that all people are players in life. Mane Tatoulian was commissioned to create the identity for the running campaign of the brand. The core idea was to show the power, velocity and energy of the runners' attitudes. Technology, innovation, strength, intelligence and movement are the key concepts. All the visual elements—colors, photography and typographic criteria—emphasize the idea behind the brand and promote its products.

Triathlon de Bordeaux

‣ Campaign

‣ DESIGN AGENCY **Studio OUAM**
‣ PHOTOGRAPHY **Triathlon de Bordeaux**

Studio OUAM created a new branding for the Triathlon of Bordeaux city (France) to give it a modern twist, which better reflects the spirit of its new team. They wanted to reach the experts but also the beginners, so this new visual communication had to be playful and simple.

TTX Creation

▸ Table Tennis Brand

▸ DESIGN AGENCY **Superunion Brand Consulting Pte Ltd**
▸ CLIENT **International Table Tennis Federation (ITTF)**

The TTX brand has been created with a lifestyle spirit at its heart, with the ambition of becoming a catalyst for disruption and high-level engagement within the category. The brand identity, "Live the Beat," uses a vibrant, multi-colored palette to convey the inclusive, diverse nature of the new format. Created for an "always-on audience," all of the elements of the identity express the spontaneous, freestyle nature of the experience and the audiences Superunion wants to attract.

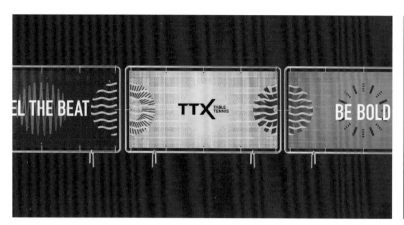

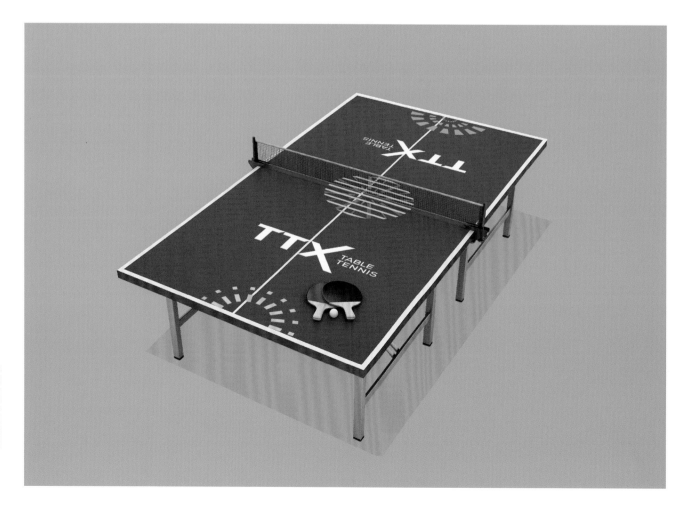

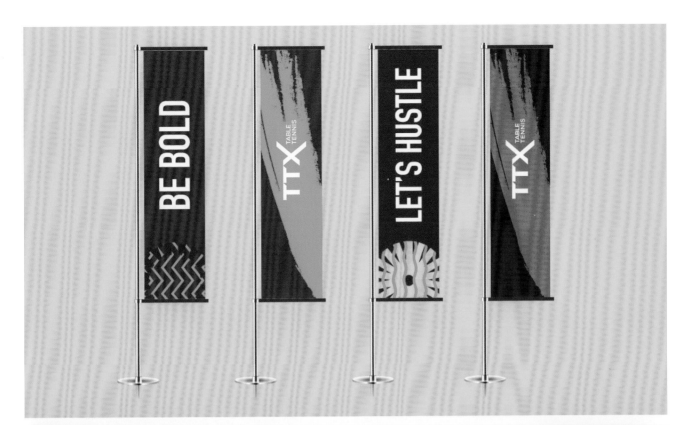

FC Mariupol

▶ Football Club

▶ DESIGN AGENCY **Sergii Dima**
▶ DESIGN **Dmitriy Silchenko**
▶ ART DIRECTION **Sergii Rodionov**
▶ MOTION DESIGN **Anastasiia Maiboroda**
▶ TYPE DESIGN **Andriy Shevchenko
  (Mariupol), type.today (Druk Wide)**
▶ PHOTOGRAPHY **NIvan Gushchin**

Sergii Dima faced a challenge to transform the middle-level Ukrainian Premier League football club, Mariupol, into a leading European team using design. They developed traditional symbols, created stylish equipment and took a holistic approach to brand communication.

Ultra X

‣ Sporting Event

‣ DESIGN AGENCY **We Launch**
‣ DESIGN **Matt Walpole, Dan Jarvis**
‣ CREATIVE DIRECTION **Stuart Lang**
‣ ACCOUNT EXECUTION **Jemma Adams**
‣ CLIENT **Jamie Sparks, Sam Heward**

Ultra X is a global sports endurance brand that wants to make multi-day foot racing accessible to all. We Launch designed the branding for the Ultra X series centered on the core values of responsible, professional, customer-centric, high-quality and persistent. The new logo, visual identity and color palette were devised to be confident, distinctive and bold, while providing an antithesis to the typically dominant colors of red and black which prevail throughout the world of endurance sport.

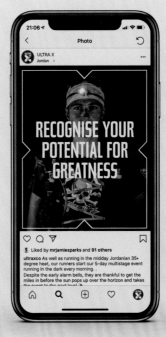

New York City Football Club Badge

‣ Football Team

‣ DESIGN AGENCY **Alfalfa Studio**
‣ DESIGN **Rafael Esquer**
‣ CLIENT **New York City Football Club**

Alfalfa Studio's Rafael Esquer designed the official badge for Major League Soccer's expansion team NYCFC in New York City. He positioned the NYCFC's badge as a genuine, authentic and timeless badge—very New York City and, at the same time, it has a presence to stand on its own in international contexts. The intertwining of the N, Y and C alludes to teamwork, strategy, harmony and unity. The circle shape, inspired by the old New York City subway token created by the Transit Authority in 1953, is a symbol of unity, wholeness, infinity, potential and the number one. The typeface, Gotham, is a wholly American font inspired by the city's signage. The colors navy blue, white and orange are drawn from the New York City flag. The light blue refers to the club's family lineage, Manchester City FC.

Juventus

▸ Football Club

▸ DESIGN AGENCY **Interbrand**
▸ CLIENT **Juventus**

Juventus, one of Italy's oldest and most beloved football clubs, aimed to distill its essence into far-reaching experiences that could appeal to football fans as well as to a wider audience. Interbrand created a logo to capture the fearlessness of Juventus that holds the visual heritage of the club while pushing towards modernity and the potential to embrace wider entertainment categories. The final result is a flexible and unmistakable system combining a unique typeface (Juventus Fans), a strong grid system, a bold photographic style system and a photographic style that is iconic, premium and unmistakable.

Rio 2016™ Olympic Games

> Sports Games

> DESIGN AGENCY **Tátil Design**

After a fierce competition, Tátil Design was selected as one of the eight finalists to create the Rio 2016 brand. Tátil Design designed a three-dimensional logo, making the local landmark come to life and gaining a three-dimensional perspective with volume and cut-outs. Its contours re-create the topography of the city. Inspired by Rio's nature, its people and the athletes, the logo of the Rio Olympic Games 2016 embodied unity, transformation, passion and energy. It's a large collective network in motion, an invitation and inspiration to Rio and the world.

Rio 2016 Emblem's Development

| First drafts with carioca's topography references and volumetric studies. | Initial emblem study, with visual reference to human figures and Sugar Loaf's shape. | Attempt to make the emblem more organic, fluid. | New study of emblem's shape, emphasizing the three human figures by making them more robust. In addition, the first volumetric study of the emblem was made with plastic dough. | Original draft of the final Rio 2016 emblem. | New draft of the final emblem, in attempt to make it more organic. | Study on the emblem's expression lines. | Study to include other shapes of Rio's topography to the emblem's curves. | Three-dimensional volumetric study made from the final emblem's shape. | Final emblem. |

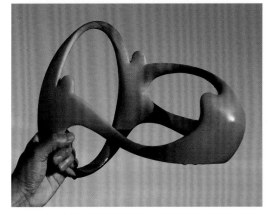

2018 Pittsburgh Marathon

▸ Sporting Event

▸ DESIGN AGENCY **Wall-to-Wall Studios**
▸ DESIGN **Nate Fussner**
▸ CREATIVE DIRECTION **Larkin Werner, Doug Dean**
▸ MOTION DESIGN **Ira Lederer**
▸ CLIENT **Pittsburgh Three Rivers Marathon, Inc.**

Pittsburgh Three Rivers Marathon, Inc. (P3R) needed a brand campaign to promote the marathon's 10th anniversary and Wall-to-Wall took on the task. The studio designed the integrated brand campaign, which included event identity and visual branding, advertising, environmental applications, apparel, social media graphics, campaign launch video, medals, style guides and more.

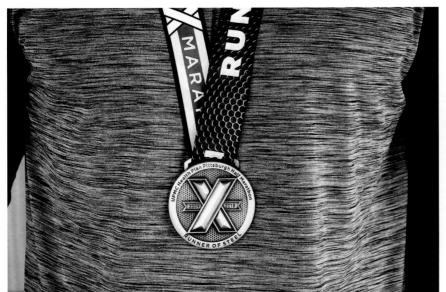

Project Happy Feet Slipper Race 2016

‣ Walking Race

‣ DESIGN AGENCY **Nout Studio**
‣ CLIENT **Project Happy Feet**

The Project Happy Feet Slipper Race was Singapore's first non-competitive walk since 2010. Nout Studio was tasked to conceptualize and execute the brand identity for the race in 2016. Their work included designing printed and digital materials, and running visuals. The happy sensation of listening to music was conveyed through the use of musical symbols and vibrant colors, and a playful and energetic vibe was brought forward to attract people of all ages to the event.

Défi Foly

▸Sporting Event

▸DESIGN AGENCY **ZGMAD**
▸DESIGN **Tommy Dorier**
▸CLIENT **Défi Foly**

The nonprofit association La Clusaz Défi Foly asked ZGMAD to create the new graphic identity for the Défi Foly, an annual "pond skimming" event in La Clusaz, France, and the advertising campaign promoting the 2018 event. The design needed to revive the popularity, interest and credibility of the event, and make it crazier, more fun, more unique, while keeping a link to the event's history, which goes back to 1980s. The client hoped the design would help the event get more support from people in town, riders, sponsors and even the non-ski enthusiasts. The design also needed to explain the ecological and altruistic aspects of the event—all the money raised was used to protect the lake and to help the young people of the community.

Asian Games 2018 Identity System and Mascot Design

▸ Sports Game

▸ DESIGN AGENCY **FEAT**
▸ DESIGN **Kristin Monica, Leonard Gani, Selly Claudia, Marvina H. Putri**
▸ CREATIVE DIRECTION **Jefferson Edri**
▸ ART DIRECTION **Kristin Monica**
▸ ILLUSTRATION **Raymond Witanto**
▸ CLIENT **Indonesian Ministry of Youth and Sports**

The competition brief stated that the visual identity and mascot should cover three criteria, Asia, Indonesia and sports, and it should represent the theme of "The Energy of Asia." Inspired by the visions and dreams of Soekarno, the first president of Indonesia, FEAT decided to use the shape of the Gelora Bung Karno Main Stadium, as the 2018 Asian Games' symbol. There were eight paths leading to the stadium and the Olympic Council of Asia's shining sun emblem in the center. And also they used "Keep the Dream Alive," as their brand story for the whole system as well as to remember President Soekarno's dream.

▾ FEAT proposed three Indonesian animals as the official game's mascots: Bhin Bhin, Papua's bird of Paradise that represents strategy; Atung, a Bawean deer that represents speed; and Kaka, the one-horned rhino from Ujung Kulon that represents power.

FC Internazionale Football Club

▸ Football Club

▸ DESIGN AGENCY **Leftloft**

FC Internazionale is a professional Italian football club based in Milan. The club, also known as Inter and as Inter Milan outside of Italy, was established in 1908 as a breakaway from AC Milan. Over the years, Inter developed a vast array of activities and divisions that needed to be renewed in a visually coherent way. The identity mixes modern elements with iconic and traditional ones. The new logo is based on Inter Milan's original 1908 pictogram, but has been modernized with fewer rings, simpler lettering, better proportions. The star above the crest, representing the number of league titles won, has been removed, but will still feature on other equipment.

▲ A series of posters was designed for FC Internazionale's campaign.
▼ The posters were hung on the wall of a shop.

Joshua Buatsi

‣ Campaign

‣ DESIGN AGENCY **Soft Power**
‣ CREATIVE DIRECTION **Jonathan Seary**
‣ PHOTOGRAPHY **Joost Vandebrug**

Soft Power was commissioned to create an identity and hyper-local campaign to promote unbeaten light heavyweight champion Joshua Buatsi in his hometown of Croydon, England. Soft Power took him to the Shrublands Estate and the Victory Boxing Club to photograph him where his story began. The campaign was to inspire young Croydeners.

▲ The logo is wrapped in reference to boxing hand wraps.

IBM Taiwan Sport Day

‣Sports Day

‣DESIGN **Yi-Hsuan Li**

The 2018 IBM Sport Day is designed with the motion pattern from ball sports as the core concept, referring to four different balls for visual development. The design depicts the outline and space of the sphere with light and shadow, and interlacing to present a mysterious and technologically-oriented visual style. Indigo represents technology and cleverness, which is set off by a black background. The light and shadows from the balls streaming across the black background create a powerful picture and a new look for IBM Sport Day.

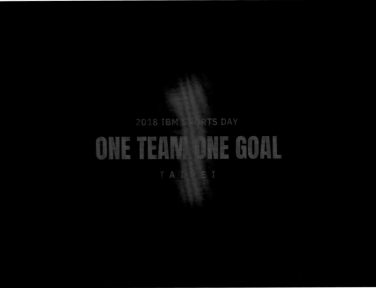

Run Mfg
▸ Event Design Studio

▸ DESIGN AGENCY **Perky Bros**
▸ CLIENT **Run Mfg**

Run Mfg is an independent race design and production studio based in Austin, Texas. Led by Nathan Barnhart and Elaine Lau, a husband and wife team, they've become known for creating unique running events with a high level of detail and creativity.

Their brand identity is made for motion. The logo, inspired by a looped shoelace, expands and contracts, building endless running routes. The simplified electric blue and black color palette creates a bold, energetic mindset and separates them from the competition, from print to digital to race day.

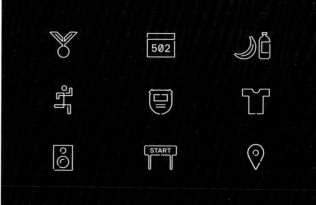

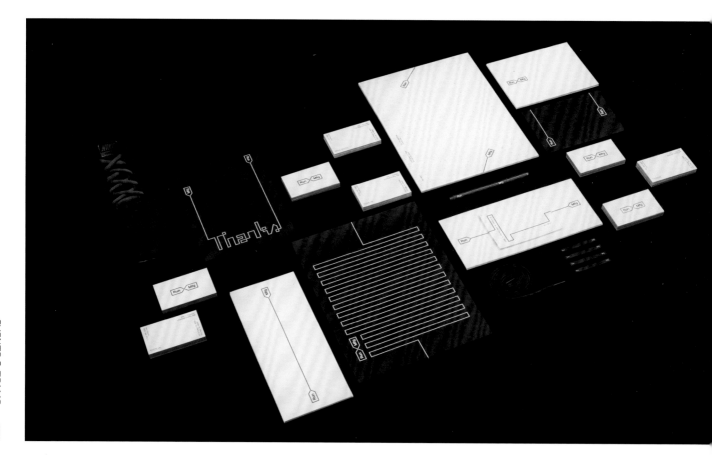

Budapest 2024 Olympics Bid Logo

‣ Bid for Olympic Games

‣ DESIGN AGENCY **Graphasel**
 Design Studio
‣ CLIENT **Budapest 2024 Nonprofit Zrt.**

The city of Budapest, Hungary submitted a bid to host the 2024 Summer Olympics. The main visual element of the bid is the logo, which the candidate cities use as a means of communication in the international press. The Budapest logo design call was announced by the Design Terminal as an open competition for designers. Graphasel Design Studio created a concept and their logo, which uses water and movement as the key elements, and it was adopted.

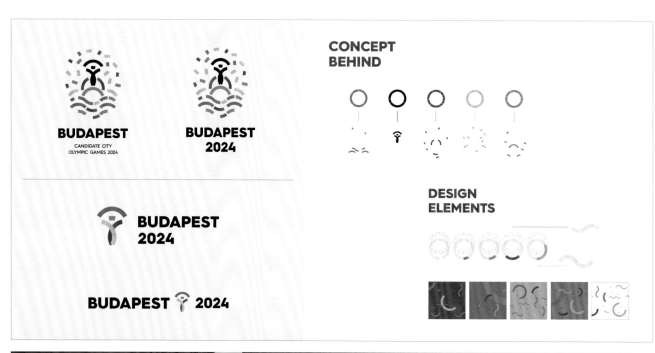

Czarni Słupsk

‣ Basketball Team

‣ DESIGN AGENCY **Rio Creativo**
‣ CLIENT **Czarni Słupsk**

Czarni Słupsk is a powerful brand with strong ties to the city of Słupsk, Poland. Rio Creativo was faced with the task of presenting the 18-year-long history of the club with all its twists and turns, in the form of a new visual identity. The new identity "Czarni is You" stems from pictures and emotions familiar to the community and strengthens the club while resonating with the surrounding environment. Also, it is not only about basketball, it's about the community and the fascinating fan stories intertwined with the team.

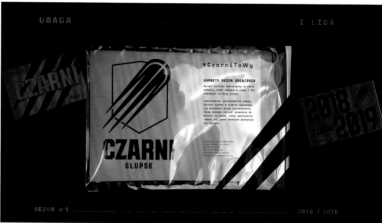

Switch Football Academy

▸ Football Team

▸ DESIGN AGENCY **Nacione™**
▸ DESIGN **Ricardo Carvalho**

Switch Football Academy is a group that is wholly committed to attaining excellence and changing the narratives currently realizable in the Nigerian football circle. The group started in 2018 and they needed a complete sports branding and identity to promote their ideas and services. They asked for a bold brand identity and sports crest using black and orange colors as guides and references. Nacione™ was responsible for developing a fresh and complete branding platform, from strategy to implementation. The project also included the creation of the shield, alternative brand versions, such as corporate, brand applications in jerseys, and variations for merchandising material, store and transportation.

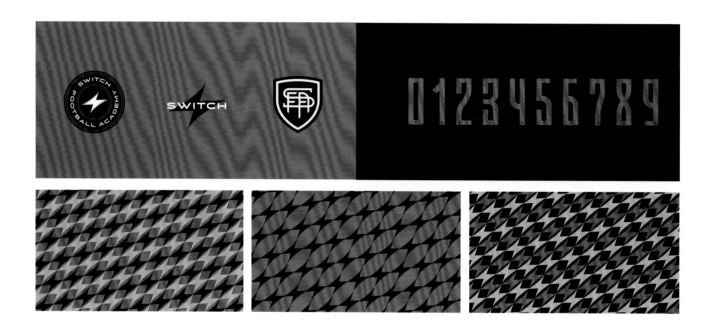

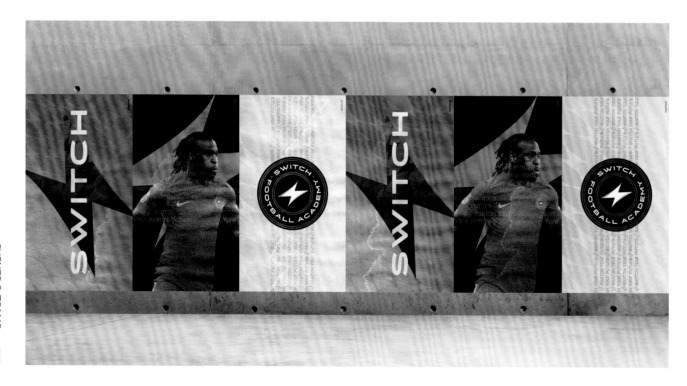

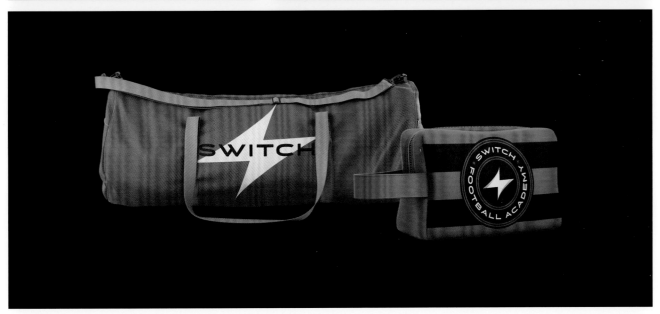

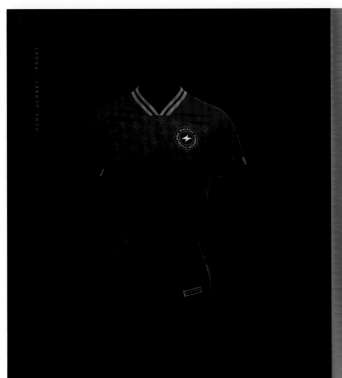

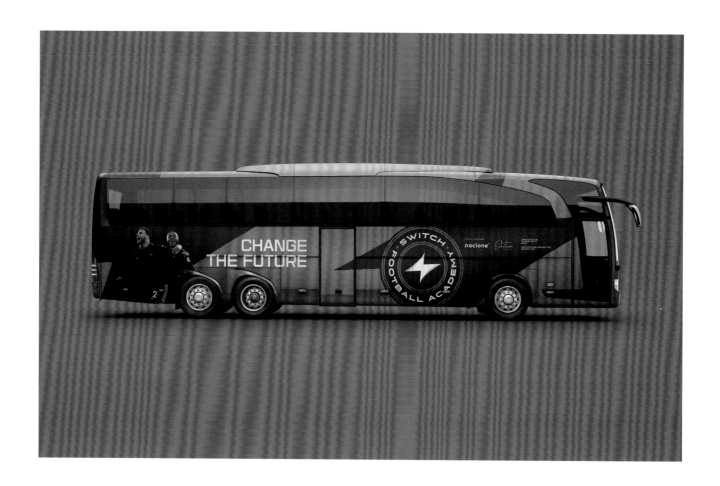

INDEX

©N7 STUDIO

©N7 STUDIO is a design and technology firm that works globally from their offices in New York, Toronto, Mexico City, and Monterrey. They strongly focus on producing high quality design and emotional brandings, digital products, and experiences for clients around the world. Their expertise is strategic brand development, UI/UX Design, and web development.

www.n7-studio.com

P038–039

9 x 9. Design

9 x 9. Design is mainly engaged in brand culture positioning, brand visual identity building, brand space planning and design, brand product incubation, and other services. They focus on designing research and process, constantly breaking the routine, using unique visual language and thinking, defamiliarization of common elements in life, transmitting visual information to customers and public, and establishing emotional expression between people and design.

www.behance.net/helloc32511b6

P092–093, 106–107

702design

702 is an experimental visual design institution. 702 has been fronting the design industry with its signature experimental approach and its vision in innovation.

www.by702.com

P056–057

Ahonen & Lamberg

Ahonen & Lamberg is a multidisciplinary design studio based in Paris. Founded in 2006 by Finnish designers Anna Ahonen and Katariina Lamberg, it concentrates on art direction, creative consultancy and graphic design covering a wide range of areas and an equally vast client list ranging from multinational companies, magazines, or luxury brands to emerging artists and fashion designers. The Ahonen & Lamberg design principle is to balance classical and alternative design, creating a tone that is always elegant, recognizable and yet eager to surprise.

www.ahonenandlamberg.com

P064–065

Alfalfa Studio

Alfalfa Studio is a branding and graphic design firm led by Rafael Esquer and located in New York City. Since 2004, Alfalfa Studio has been creating truly inspiring work for brands in sports, culture and entertainment. Their philosophy is making the idea clear and simple.

www.alfalfastudio.com

P204–205

Anagrama Studio

Anagrama is an international branding, architecture and software development firm with offices in Monterrey and Mexico City. Their clients include companies from varied industries in countries all around the world. Besides their history and experience with brand development, they are also experts in the design and development of objects, spaces, software and multimedia projects. Anagrama breaks from the traditional creative agency scheme, integrating multidisciplinary teams of creative and business experts.

www.anagrama.com

P030–031

Animal

Animal is an independent creative agency based in New Delhi and New York with a focus on strategy in advertising and design.

www.weareanimal.co

P170–171

Apus Agency

Apus Agency has a wide range of experience in visual and digital identity. Their goal is to launch sharp brands and functional digital projects that solve client's problems.

www.apus.agency

P088–089

artless Inc.

artless Inc. is a global branding agency integrating graphics and architecture, based in Tokyo and Kyoto. It was founded by Shun Kawakami in 2001. Their activities are based in visual communication and the language of design. They specialize in branding and consulting, art and design, graphics and identity, architecture and interior, typography and signage, fashion and music, web and digital experience, advertising and brand communications.

www.artless.co.jp

P134–135

Ascend Studio

Ascend Studio is a full-service brand and design agency based in London, UK. Their work is defined by clear vision and expressed through concepts that are strategically led and objectively measured. Working collaboratively with clients, they craft brand purpose into meaningful narratives through form, function and style.

www.ascendstudio.co.uk

P140–141

Belen Ramos

Belen Ramos is a designer from Buenos Aires currently enjoying the slower pace of Hobart, Tasmania. With over 10 years of experience in the industry, she believes in the importance of conceptual thinking—and the value it brings to any project, large or small. Today she runs her own business providing a specialized service primarily in the areas of branding, editorial design and packaging, with a passion for crafted typography and bold color palettes.

www.belu.design

P142–143

BGN

BGN is a branding agency that works with businesses to maximize their potential with effective design across all platforms. Working with household brands and start-ups alike, BGN creates disruptive brand experiences that actually deliver results.

www.bgn.agency

P124–125

Blürb Studio

Blürb is a design studio oriented on creating and implementing advanced branding strategies. They help to define new brands, reshape and develop those that already existed; they facilitate brands in reaching their target audiences and support them in the improvement of their mutual relations.

www.blurbstudio.com

P188–189

Bold Scandinavia

Strategic design agency Bold Scandinavia is a member of The North Alliance. They have offices in Sweden, Denmark and Norway.

www.boldscandinavia.com

P149

Brand Brothers

Brand Brothers is a brand design studio. They do brand strategy, visual identity and branding. They've worked from Paris and Toulouse since 2010, for emerging startups as well as for centenary groups. Driven by curiosity, transmission, reflection and new challenges, they aim to produce useful, intelligible and beautiful design for companies, brands and virtuous people.

www.brandbrothers.fr

P160–162

Brandon Archibald

Brandon Archibald is a branding, architecture and interior design agency. They help clients to develop concept, name, logo, corporate identity, interior and exterior design. Their clients come from completely different countries, of different races and religions, traditions, customs and time zones.

www.brandon-archibald.com

P120–121

Brands&People

Brands&People is a brand-centric company focused on mobilizing commercial brands in Latin America. They steer, innovate, communicate and maximize brands to accelerate growth.

www.brands.mx

P020–021

Bravo

Bravo is a creatively led, independent design studio based in Singapore. They work with a variety of individuals and organizations to deliver considered and engaging design. They specialize in identity and brand creation, print and web communication, and art direction.

www.bravo.rocks

P126–127

Bruce Mau Design

Bruce Mau Design is a multidisciplinary brand design firm working worldwide with organizations shaping the future of their respective industries.

www.brucemaudesign.com

P068–069

byHAUS

byHAUS is the design studio of Philippe Archontakis and Martin Laliberté, two accredited graphic designers based in Montreal. The studio specializes in creating distinctive identities that drive success.

www.byhaus.ca

P032–033

Chapter Branding Studio

Chapter is a design studio based in Mexico. They focus on the inner core of creating a brand, trusting the design as an end result will be beautiful, coherent and timeless. Also, they believe the brand strategy and personality are key components that need to exist within each behavior and application of the brand.

www.chapter.mx

P066–067

Code Switch

Code Switch is an award-winning design studio based in Northampton, Massachusetts. Code Switch is run by Jan Šabach, a Czech-born graphic designer and creative director.

www.codeswitchdesign.com

P182–183

Crate47

Crate47 is a vibrant British design agency based in both London and Brighton, offering strategically creative solutions in branding, web design and content creation. Being experts in these three core areas means that they can maintain continuity across all areas of a brand, ensuring a consistent visual identity and a strong overall message.

www.crate47.com

P042–043

Daniel Ting Chong

Daniel Ting Chong is a designer and illustrator based in Cape Town, South Africa. Daniel was born in 1987 in Cape Town and is a third generation South African Chinese. After studying graphic design at Vega School, he is emerging as one of Cape Town's top creative talents following a series of commissions from clients and design collaborations with leading international brands including Nike, New York Times and PUMA.

www.danieltingchong.com

P052–053, 060–061

Departamento

Departamento is a design studio between Monterrey and Mexico City that develops creative brands. Their philosophy leads to an individual scheme development for every client. Keeping in mind that essential principles of design help amplify unique assets and build leading brands among the market.

www.departamento.design

P044–045

Dima Goreniuk

Dima Goreniuk is a graphic designer and art director based in Kyiv, Ukraine. Currently, he is part of a graphic design duo called Jugoceania.

www.jaydimma.com

P194–195

Dragon Rouge

Dragon Rouge is a global creative agency that fuses original insight and creative flair to deliver breakthrough strategy, design and innovation. From their eight offices, Paris, London, Hamburg, Warsaw, New York, Sao Paulo, Shanghai and Singapore, they design for brands with bold ideas and brave hearts.

www.dragonrouge.com

P178–181, 190–191

ED.

ED. is an Australian digital studio that builds beautiful brands and websites. They work hand in hand with their clients through their unique, collaborative design process to create iconic, memorable and boundary-pushing work.

www.ed.com.au

P028–029, 144

Ehrhorn Hummerston

Ehrhorn Hummerston is a design and communication agency situated in the heart of Copenhagen, Denmark. From there, they help clients from all over the world unfold their full potential digitally and in print.

www.eh.dk

P136–137

Estudio Yeyé

Estudio Yeyé is a Mexico-based creative studio specialized in graphic design, photography, publicity and illustration. Their principal goal is to give their clients work that is relevant, innovative and of utmost quality to help their business grow.

www.yeye.design

P086-087

Fable

Fable is an award-winning, multi-disciplinary design consultancy that designs brand strategies, visual identities, creative campaigns, print and digital communications, spatial experiences and more. They were recognized at established international design competitions, such as the prestigious British Design & Art Direction Awards and the Tokyo Type Directors Club.

www.fable.sg

P096-097

FEAT

FEAT is a small graphic design studio in Jakarta, Indonesia. They work with brands to help them connect to their audience with the use of visual identity systems, brand communication, editorial and printed matter.

www.featstudio.com

P216-219

FLUORO.

Clean, minimal, and bold thinking is what sets FLUORO. up in world of contemporary culture. Their work speaks as much through what is left out as what is included. This holds true across their broad range of commissions, from high fashion brands and leading sports apparel, to the worlds' finest arts institutions.

www.fluoro.london

P138-139

Forth + Back

Forth + Back is a multidisciplinary design studio based in Los Angeles, founded by Nikolos Killian and Tanner Woodbury. Together, they view their studio as a platform to break ground in problems old and new. The studio aspires to stay curious and continually share their curiosities with others.

www.forthandback.la

P040-041

Frost*collective

Frost* is a collective of strategists, built-environment specialists, digital innovators and highly creative designers who are dedicated to designing a better world with every project. They offer the benefits of collaboration across the Frost*collective, which is at the intersection of digital, physical and visual experiences.

www.frostcollective.com.au

P082-083

Futura

Futura is an independent, multi-disciplinary design agency based in Joburg, South Africa. They create concepts, experiences, interactions and communication for a new generation of consumers. They believe in the transformative power of good design.

www.futura.co.za

P010-015, 168-169

Go4Gold

Go4Gold is a digital and online marketing studio in the field of sports based in Prague, Czech Republic.

www.go4gold.cz

P172-173

Graphasel Design Studio

Graphasel Design Studio's mission is to provide their clients with visual concepts, conceived with the highest artistic quality. They always want to create more than mere design, and strive to find the best possible means of implementation. Their goal is to build well-functioning visual communications projects that have as much creative appeal as purpose. They are open to new challenges that require unique graphic design solutions online and offline platforms alike.

www.graphasel.com

P226-227

GRDN

GRDN is a design studio from Quebec City. The collective supports organizations in their transformation by placing the human at the heart of its approach. Their process rethinks the customer relationship by offering solutions that have a real impact.

grdn.studio

P184-185

hatem + d

Established in 1998, hatem + d is a multi-disciplinary agency based in Quebec City. Specialized in branding, this company has crafted a creative ecosystem where strategy, design, digital, customer-experience and architecture connect to create strong brands.

www.hatem.ca

P152-153

Heavy

Heavy is a design studio based in Guadalajara, Mexico that focuses on branding and corporate identity. Heavy brands are created by building a narrative and core concept that the target can relate to, and even fall in love with. They perceive brands as people with character, taste and aspirations. Their method relies on a balance of emotional and aesthetic values that translates into strong positioning in a given market and recognition within the target audience.

www.heavy.mx

P036-037

ico Design

ico Design is a London-based design studio that creates and builds memorable brands for businesses and organizations with ambition.

www.icodesign.com

P058

Interbrand

Interbrand is a leading global brand consultancy, with a network of thinkers, makers and collaborators. Over the past four decades, Interbrand have pioneered iconic work and invented many of the brand building tools that are industry standards. Regarded as the university of branding, Interbrand developed the Best Global Brands ranking, have published 18 books that are often the reference point for university curriculum and professional associations, and established academy for accelerated learning in the marketing world.

www.interbrand.com

P206-207

My Name Is Wendy

My Name Is Wendy was born in 2006. The group produces brand identities, typefaces, illustrations, motion designs, patterns, typographical compositions and visual concepts. They work with clients from the cultural world, with independent projects, small companies and multi-national brands.

www.mynameiswendy.fr

P022–023

Nacione™

Nacione™ started its operation in 2014 creating and developing brand identities and strategies for football clubs who wanted to update and rethink their image and reputation. Since then, they developed brands and projects for different sports around the world like baseball, hockey, football, American football and racing teams. Today Nacione™ is a creative partner for the sports, entertainment and tourism industries.

www.nacione.com

P230–232

Nothing Design Studio

Nothing Design is an independent graphic design and branding studio. They offer strategy, art direction and design across all platforms.

www.madebynothing.com

P116–117

Nout Studio

Nout is a graphic design studio that aims to create disruption and break patterns. Combining storytelling and design, they have a critical focus on constructing brand authenticity and identity to channel and communicate their client's core messages.

www.noutstudio.com

P212–213

Oh Yeah Studio

Oh Yeah Studio was established in 2009 in Oslo and run by Hans Christian Øren. OYS works widely within the design disciplines and has clients like Nike, Adobe, UNICEF, Adidas, ESPN and Burton.

www.ohyeahstudio.no

P070–071

Onwards

Onwards is a London-based brand and design agency for scaling startups. They help founders and their teams build bold and personality-packed brands that supercharge growth.

www.onwards.agency

P062–063

papa tom

Design agency papa tom is a collective of creative thinkers, digital developers and strategists. They advise, create identities and content, develop websites and make things tangible.

www.papatom.studio

P118–119

Parámetro Studio

Parámetro Studio is a design studio located in Monterrey, Mexico focused on creating new and iconic brands.

www.parametrostudio.com

P104–105

Perky Bros

The Nashville-based design studio Perky Bros exists to help brands gain clarity, value, and distinction through design. They create visual identities, websites, packaging and print materials. Working with start-ups to more established brands, they like to keep their approach flexible. They strive to offer solutions built on plain-spoken, ambitious ideas—always grounded in research and meticulously crafted in their execution.

www.perkybros.com

P224–225

Plus X

Plus X is a brand experience marketing and design partner. The company was founded in July 2010 by five people. Currently, Shin Myungsup and Byun Sabum are running the company together. They aim for the best design output that any business would seek for marketing in diverse media and delivering an accurate user experience.

www.plus-ex.com

P146–147

Ramona Katcheika Paloschi

Ramona Katcheika Paloschi is a Brazil-based graphic designer specializing in identity development and digital retouching.

www.behance.net/katheika

P150–151

Re Agency

Re delivers brand and design services from offices in Sydney, London, Shanghai and soon to be in New York. As part of the M&C Saatchi global network, Re has defined and designed brands for some of the world's largest organizations. Services include brand design, experience design and organization design.

www.re.agency

P018–019

ReflexDesign

ReflexDesign is a design and innovation studio. They provide design and consultation services for customers in different industries. They believe the nature of the brand is a conditioned reflection. They search for insight, solve problems and build attractions. Their work is to help brands establish and enhance such connections through innovative design.

www.reflexdesign.cn

P114–115

Rio Creativo

Rio Creativo is a design studio focused on branding and visual communication. Rio is also a place where different perspectives, points of view and ideas have been crossing paths for 10 years.

www.riocreativo.pl

P228–229

Rosie Lee

Rosie Lee is a creative agency with expertise in design, creative, digital and consultancy. It was founded in UK in 2001, and now has four studios worldwide.

rosieleecreative.com

P076–081

The Birthdays Design

The Birthdays Design is founded in 2013 in Athens, Greece. The office operates locally and abroad, on art direction and graphic design for print and digital mediums, for commercial and cultural sector. The office shares time between commissioned projects and academic research.

www.thebirthdaysdesign.com

P046 -047

The Hungry Design Co.

The Hungry Design Co. is a graphic design and illustration studio based in Mexico.

thehungry.mx

P048-049

Tiffanie Mazellier

Tiffanie is a graphic designer and art director from Nouméa, New Caledonia. Studied graphic design in France, she specializes in branding and visual identity with a keen eye for typography and loves to try and think out of the box. Tiffanie works as a freelancer but loves to team up with other independents to come up with new and innovating stuff and push the boundaries.

www.behance.net/tiffaniemazellier

P102-103

Touch

Touch is an independent graphic design studio based in Edinburgh, Scotland. They make sense of things for brands, people and places. From brand identity and design for print to website projects, everything they do is carefully considered and expertly crafted. Their expertise lies in design, direction and ideas.

www.thetouchagency.co.uk

P130-131

Tyodi Hyojin Lee

Tyodi Hyojin Lee is a brand experience designer in Seoul, South Korea. He attempts to deliver the differentiated brand experience by boundlessly agonizing at the various intersections of brand and customers. He makes diverse graphic-and-illustration-based attempts, including branding, based on antique things, new things, experience and value.

www.tyo-stitch.com

P016-017

vegrande®

vegrande® designs solutions for brands starting by forging a strong relationship with every client based on mutual trust and understanding. The heart of their work is a constant strive for applying innovative design solutions, balancing an artistic sensibility with the available media, materials and handiwork—through analytic, critique, planning, quotation and supervision processes.

www.vegrande.com

P122-123

VMLY&R

VMLY&R is a global brand experience agency that harnesses creativity, technology and culture to create connected brands.

www.vml.com

P186-187

VOLTA Brand Shaping Studio

VOLTA is an independent branding and design studio based in Porto, Portugal. They design meaningful, immersive brands and integrate different disciplines to overcome communication and design problems. With a focus on branding, packaging and product design, their goal is to create true and impactful brand experiences that will set the brand, its promise and products apart from its competitors and closer to its audience.

www.volta.pt

P034-035, 098-101

Wall-to-Wall Studios

Wall-to-Wall Studios is a full-service integrated brand design agency founded in 1992. Their work spans many verticals. They have experience representing the full emotional and aesthetic spectrum. Their clients are diverse—big, small, and in-between, local, regional, and national. They believe in creating compelling integrated experiences for smart challenger brands.

www.walltowall.com

P210-211

We Launch

We Launch is a brand business that helps organizations deliver commercial success, change perceptions and empower cultural impact through their brand. Proud to be considered one of the Top 100 brand consultancies in the UK, their work spans every industry sector—across multiple continents.

www.welaunch.co.uk

P202-203

Yi-Hsuan Li

Yi-Hsuan Li is a problem-solving visual designer focusing on print and screen-based design—branding, typography, packaging, web and app design. She specializes in minimalist and eastern design styles. She always engages in designs combined with traditional and modern elements to offer a different view with her special aesthetic experience.

www.studiopros.work

P223

Yorgo&Co.

Yorgo&Co. is a multi-disciplinary design studio based in Paris, cofounded by Yorgo Tloupas and Emmanuelle Beaudet.

www.yorgo.co

P132-133

ZGMAD

ZGMAD is a marketing firm headquartered in Aspen, Colorado serving clients worldwide. They provide large-agency expertise at an intimate scale, with powerful branding at the core of each project.

zgmad.com

P214-215

ACKNOWLEDGMENTS

We would like to express our gratitude to all of the designers and companies for their generous contribution of images, ideas and concepts. We are also very grateful to many other people whose names do not appear in the credits, but who made specific contributions and provided support. Without them, the successful compilation of this book would not have been possible. Special thanks to all of the contributors for sharing their innovation and creativity with all of our readers around the world.